Credits

Author
Chandramani Tiwary

Reviewers
Saleem A. Ansari

Sahil Kharb

Pavan Kumar Narayanan

Commissioning Editor
Akram Hussain

Acquisition Editor
Sonali Vernekar

Content Development Editor
Arun Nadar

Technical Editors
Narsimha Pai

Mitali Somaiya

Copy Editors
Charlotte Carneiro

Merilyn Pereira

Vikrant Phadke

Project Coordinator
Nikhil Nair

Proofreaders
Simran Bhogal

Safis Editing

Indexer
Mariammal Chettiyar

Graphics
Sheetal Aute

Disha Haria

Abhinash Sahu

Production Coordinator
Manu Joseph

Cover Work
Manu Joseph

About the Author

Chandramani Tiwary is a Data Scientist with special interest towards building data driven products. He is a founding member of the Data Science team at Gainsight and was instrumental in framing Data Science use cases for customer success management in the SaaS industry. He is also an advisor to multiple organizations. He can be followed on Twitter at https://twitter.com/Mani_on_Twitt and on LinkedIn at https://www.linkedin.com/today/author/60666042.

I would like to take this opportunity to thank my parents and my brother for always trusting and encouraging me; I wouldn't have been where I am without their support. I would also like to thank Packt Publishing, the various editors, and the reviewers of this book for their efforts in making this book possible.

Learning Apache Mahout

Acquire practical skills in Big Data Analytics and explore data science with Apache Mahout

Chandramani Tiwary

PUBLISHING

BIRMINGHAM - MUMBAI

Learning Apache Mahout

Copyright © 2015 Packt Publishing

First published: March 2015

Production reference: 2071215

Published by Packt Publishing Ltd.
Livery Place
35 Livery Street
Birmingham B3 2PB, UK.

ISBN 978-1-78355-521-5

www.packtpub.com

About the Reviewers

Saleem A. Ansari is a full-stack Java, Scala, and Ruby developer with over 7 years of industry experience and a special interest in machine learning and information retrieval. Having implemented the data ingestion and processing pipeline in Core Java and Ruby separately, he knows the challenges faced by huge datasets in such systems. He has worked for companies such as Red Hat, Impetus Technologies, Belzabar Software, and Exzeo Software. He is also a passionate member of the Free and Open Source Software (FOSS) community. He started his journey with FOSS in 2004. The very next year, 2005, he formed JMILUG, a Linux user group at Jamia Millia Islamia University, New Delhi. Since then, he has been contributing to FOSS by organizing community activities and contributing code to various projects (such as github.com/tuxdna). He also advises students about FOSS and its benefits. He is currently enrolled at Georgia Institute of Technology, USA, for the MSCS program. He can be reached at tuxdna@fedoraproject.org. He maintains a blog at http://tuxdna.in/.

First of all, I would like to thank the vibrant, talented, and very generous Apache Mahout community, who created such a wonderful machine learning library. I would like to thank Packt Publishing and its staff for giving me this wonderful opportunity. I would also like to thank the author for his hard work in simplifying and elaborating the latest developments in Apache Mahout.

Sahil Kharb is the computer science undergraduate student at Indian Institute of Technology, Jodhpur (India). He has been working on Mahout and Hadoop for the last 2 years. His area of interest is data mining on a large scale. Nowadays, he works on Apache Spark and Apache Storm, doing real-time data analytics and batch processing with the help of Apache Mahout.

> I would like to thank my family who always supported me in learning new technologies and also my friends Mohit Dadhich, Prashant Mittal, Manish Sachdeva, and Pratik Kumar, who helped me in testing codes.

Pavan Kumar Narayanan is an applied mathematician with experience in mathematical programming, Data Science, and scientific computing projects. He has published and presented papers on applied mathematics in Washington DC and New York, and also maintains a blog, DataScience Hacks (`https://datasciencehacks.wordpress.com/`). Currently, he is a graduate student in computational mathematics in New York. He loves exploring new problem solving techniques and software, from industrial mathematics to machine learning, in addition to reviewing Packt Publishing books.

> I would like to thank my family for their unconditional love and support and God almighty for giving me strength and endurance.

www.PacktPub.com

Support files, eBooks, discount offers, and more

For support files and downloads related to your book, please visit www.PacktPub.com.

Did you know that Packt offers eBook versions of every book published, with PDF and ePub files available? You can upgrade to the eBook version at www.PacktPub.com and as a print book customer, you are entitled to a discount on the eBook copy. Get in touch with us at service@packtpub.com for more details.

At www.PacktPub.com, you can also read a collection of free technical articles, sign up for a range of free newsletters and receive exclusive discounts and offers on Packt books and eBooks.

https://www2.packtpub.com/books/subscription/packtlib

Do you need instant solutions to your IT questions? PacktLib is Packt's online digital book library. Here, you can search, access, and read Packt's entire library of books.

Why subscribe?

- Fully searchable across every book published by Packt
- Copy and paste, print, and bookmark content
- On demand and accessible via a web browser

Free access for Packt account holders

If you have an account with Packt at www.PacktPub.com, you can use this to access PacktLib today and view 9 entirely free books. Simply use your login credentials for immediate access.

Table of Contents

Preface

Learning Apache Mahout is aimed at providing a strong foundation in machine learning using Mahout. This book is ideal for learning the core concepts of machine learning and the basics of Mahout. This book will go from the basics of Mahout and machine learning, to feature engineering and the implementation of various machine learning algorithms in Mahout. Algorithm usage examples will be explained using both the Mahout command line and its Java API. We will conclude the book with two chapters of end-to-end case studies. Ideally, chapters 1, 2 and 3 should be read sequentially, chapters 4 to 8 in any order, and chapters 9 and 10 after chapter 1 to 8 have been completed.

What this book covers

Chapter 1, Introduction to Mahout, covers the setup of the learning environment, installation, and the configuration of the various tools required for this book. It will discuss the need for a machine learning library such as Mahout and introduce the basics of Mahout with command line and code examples.

Chapter 2, Core Concepts in Machine Learning, covers the fundamental concepts in machine learning. It will discuss the important steps involved in a machine learning project, such as data processing, model training, and efficacy, and provides an intuitive explanation of different algorithms.

Chapter 3, Feature Engineering, covers the most important phase of a machine learning project, feature extraction and representation. It will discuss common data preprocessing tasks, manual and automated feature transformation, feature selection, and dimensionality reduction.

Chapter 4, Classification with Mahout, covers classification algorithms implemented in Mahout. It will discuss the important phases of building a classifier, such as preprocessing data, creating a train and test set, and measuring model efficacy. The algorithms that will be covered are logistic regression, random forest, and naïve Bayes.

Chapter 5, Frequent Pattern Mining and Topic Modeling, covers algorithms for frequent pattern mining and topic modeling. This chapter will provide an intuitive explanation of the algorithms and include both command line and code examples, while also providing practical examples.

Chapter 6, Recommendation with Mahout, covers algorithms to build recommender systems in Mahout. It will discuss item-based and user-based recommenders. This chapter will provide an intuitive explanation of the algorithms and include both command line and code examples, while also providing practical examples.

Chapter 7, Clustering with Mahout, covers algorithms to perform clustering in Mahout. It will discuss algorithms such as k-means, fuzzy k-means, streaming k-means, and so on. This chapter will provide an intuitive explanation of the algorithm and include both command line and code examples, while also providing practical examples.

Chapter 8, New Paradigm in Mahout, covers the porting of Mahout on top of Apache Spark. It will discuss the installation and configuration of Mahout and Spark, explain the important concepts of Spark and Mahout binding, and cover some basic examples.

Chapter 9, Case Study – Churn Analytics and Customer Segmentation, covers the steps involved in a machine learning project from start to finish. It will discuss all the important steps that need to be performed for a successful machine learning project. It will take a couple of use cases from customer analytics, churn analytics, and customer segmentation, to walk through the process.

Chapter 10, Case Study – Text Analytics, covers the steps involved in a text analytics project. It will discuss the vector space model of representing text, text clustering, and classification.

What you need for this book

For this book, you will need the following software:

- Java 1.6 or higher
- Maven 2.0 or higher
- Hadoop 1.2.1

- Eclipse with Maven plug-in
- Mahout 0.9
- Python
- R

We will cover every software needed for this book in the corresponding chapters. All the examples in the book have been coded using the Ubuntu 12.04 LTS release.

Who this book is for

If you are a Java developer and want to use Mahout and machine learning to solve Big Data Analytics use cases, then this book is ideal for you. This book is good for self-learners who want to learn the fundamental concepts of machine learning and the practical implementations of Mahout. Some familiarity with shell scripts, Python, and R is assumed, but no prior experience is required.

Conventions

In this book, you will find a number of styles of text that distinguish between different kinds of information. Here are some examples of these styles, and an explanation of their meaning.

Code words in text, database table names, folder names, filenames, file extensions, pathnames, dummy URLs, user input, and Twitter handles are shown as follows: "The output of the `sed` command is saved to the new file `adult.data.csv`."

Any command-line input or output is written as follows:

```
sudo pip install pandas
```

New terms and **important words** are shown in bold. Words that you see on the screen, in menus or dialog boxes for example, appear in the text like this: "Once the search results are displayed hit **Install** and follow the instructions."

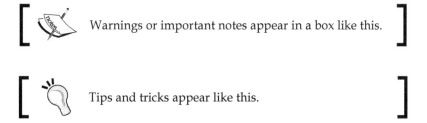

> Warnings or important notes appear in a box like this.

> Tips and tricks appear like this.

Reader feedback

Feedback from our readers is always welcome. Let us know what you think about this book—what you liked or may have disliked. Reader feedback is important for us to develop titles that you really get the most out of.

To send us general feedback, simply send an e-mail to feedback@packtpub.com, and mention the book title via the subject of your message.

If there is a topic that you have expertise in and you are interested in either writing or contributing to a book, see our author guide on www.packtpub.com/authors.

Customer support

Now that you are the proud owner of a Packt book, we have a number of things to help you to get the most from your purchase.

Downloading the example code

You can download the example code files for all Packt books you have purchased from your account at http://www.packtpub.com. If you purchased this book elsewhere, you can visit http://www.packtpub.com/support and register to have the files e-mailed directly to you.

Errata

Although we have taken every care to ensure the accuracy of our content, mistakes do happen. If you find a mistake in one of our books—maybe a mistake in the text or the code—we would be grateful if you would report this to us. By doing so, you can save other readers from frustration and help us improve subsequent versions of this book. If you find any errata, please report them by visiting http://www.packtpub.com/submit-errata, selecting your book, clicking on the **errata submission form** link, and entering the details of your errata. Once your errata are verified, your submission will be accepted and the errata will be uploaded on our website, or added to any list of existing errata, under the Errata section of that title. Any existing errata can be viewed by selecting your title from http://www.packtpub.com/support.

Piracy

Piracy of copyright material on the Internet is an ongoing problem across all media. At Packt, we take the protection of our copyright and licenses very seriously. If you come across any illegal copies of our works, in any form, on the Internet, please provide us with the location address or website name immediately so that we can pursue a remedy.

Please contact us at copyright@packtpub.com with a link to the suspected pirated material.

We appreciate your help in protecting our authors, and our ability to bring you valuable content.

Questions

You can contact us at questions@packtpub.com if you are having a problem with any aspect of the book, and we will do our best to address it.

1
Introduction to Mahout

Mahout is an open source machine learning library from Apache. Mahout primarily implements clustering, recommender engines (collaborative filtering), classification, and dimensionality reduction algorithms but is not limited to these.

The aim of Mahout is to provide a scalable implementation of commonly used machine learning algorithms. Mahout is the machine learning tool of choice if the data to be used is large. What we generally mean by large is that the data cannot be processed on a single machine. With Big Data becoming an important focus area, Mahout fulfils the need for a machine learning tool that can scale beyond a single machine. The focus on scalability differentiates Mahout from other tools such as R, Weka, and so on.

The learning implementations in Mahout are written in Java, and major portions, but not all, are built upon Apache's Hadoop distributed computation project using the MapReduce paradigm. Efforts are on to build Mahout on Apache Spark using Scala DSL. Programs written in Scala DSL will be automatically optimized and executed in parallel on Apache Spark. Commits of new algorithms in MapReduce have been stopped and the existing MapReduce implementation will be supported.

The purpose of this chapter is to understand the fundamental concepts behind Mahout. In particular, we will cover the following topics:

- Why Mahout
- When Mahout
- How Mahout

Why Mahout

We already have many good open source machine learning software tools. The statistical language R has a very large community, good IDE, and a large collection of machine learning packages already implemented. Python has a strong community and is multipurpose, and in Java we have Weka.

So what is the need for a new machine learning framework?

The answer lies in the scale of data. Organizations are generating terabytes of data daily and there is a need for a machine learning framework that can process that amount of data.

That begs a question, can't we just sample the data and use existing tools for our analytics use cases?

Simple techniques and more data is better

Collecting and processing data is much easier today than, say, a decade ago. IT infrastructure has seen an enormous improvement; ETL tools, click stream providers such as Google analytics, stream processing frameworks such as Kafka, Storm, and so on have made collecting data much easier. Platforms like Hadoop, Cassandra, and MPP databases such as Teradata have made storing and processing huge amount of data much easier than earlier. From a large-scale production algorithm standpoint, we have seen that simpler algorithms on very large amounts of data produce reasonably good results.

Sampling is difficult

Sampling may lead to over-fitting and increases the complexity of preparing data to build models to solve the problem at hand. Though sampling tends to simplify things by allowing scientists to work on a small sample instead of the whole population and helps in using existing tools like R to scale up to the task, getting a representative sample is tricky.

I'd say when you have the choice of getting more data, take it. Never discard data. Throw more (commodity) hardware at the data by using platforms and tools such as Hadoop and Mahout.

Community and license

Another advantage of Mahout is its license. Mahout is Apache licensed, which means that you can incorporate pieces of it into your own software regardless of whether you want to release your source code. However, other ML software, such as Weka, are under the GPL license, which means that incorporating them into your software forces you to release source code for any software you package with Weka components.

When Mahout

We have discussed the advantages of using Mahout, let's now discuss the scenarios where using Mahout is a good choice.

Data too large for single machine

If the data is too large to process on a single machine then it would be a good starting point to think about a distributed system. Rather than scaling and buying bigger hardware, it could be a better option to scale out, buy more machines, and distribute the processing.

Data already on Hadoop

A lot of enterprises have adopted Hadoop as their Big Data platform and have used it to store and aggregate data. Mahout has been designed to run algorithms on top of Hadoop and has a relatively straightforward configuration.

If your data or the bulk of it is already on Hadoop, then Mahout is a natural choice to run machine learning algorithms.

Algorithms implemented in Mahout

Do check whether the use case that needs to be implemented has a corresponding algorithm implemented in Mahout, or you have the required expertise to extend Mahout to implement your own algorithms.

How Mahout

In this section, you will learn how to install and configure Mahout.

Setting up the development environment

For any development work involving Mahout, and to follow the examples in this book, you will require the following setup:

- Java 1.6 or higher
- Maven 2.0 or higher
- Hadoop 1.2.1
- Eclipse with Maven plugin
- Mahout 0.9

I prefer to try out the latest version, barring when there are known compatibility issues. To configure Hadoop, follow the instructions on this page http://hadoop. apache.org/docs/r1.2.1/single_node_setup.html. We will focus on configuring Maven, Eclipse with the Maven plugin, and Mahout.

Configuring Maven

Maven can be downloaded from one of the mirrors of the Apache website http:// maven.apache.org/download.cgi. We use Apache Maven 3.2.5 and the same can be downloaded using this command:

```
wget http://apache.mirrors.tds.net/maven/maven-3/3.2.5/binaries/apache-
maven-3.2.5-bin.tar.gz
cd /usr/local
sudo tar xzf $HOME/Downloads/ /usr/local/apache-maven-3.2.5-bin.tar.gz
sudo mv apache-maven-3.2.5 maven
sudo chown -R $USER maven
```

Configuring Mahout

Mahout can be configured to be run with or without Hadoop. Currently, efforts are on to port Mahout on Apache Spark but it is in a nascent stage. We will discuss Mahout on Spark in *Chapter 8, New Paradigm in Mahout*. In this chapter, you are going to learn how to configure Mahout on top of Hadoop.

We will have two configurations for Mahout. The first we will use for practicing command line examples of Mahout and the other, compiled from source, will be used to develop Mahout code using Java API and Eclipse.

Though we can use one Mahout configuration, I will take this opportunity to discuss both approaches.

Download the latest Mahout version using one of the mirrors listed at the Apache Mahout website https://mahout.apache.org/general/downloads.html. The current release version is mahout-distribution-0.9.tar.gz. After the download completes, the archive should be in the Downloads folder under the user's home directory. Type the following on the command line. The first command moves the shell prompt to the /usr/local directory:

```
cd /usr/local
```

Extract the downloaded file to the directory mahout-distribution-0.9.tar.gz under the /usr/local directory. The command tar is used to extract the archive:

```
sudo tar xzf $HOME/Downloads/mahout-distribution-0.9.tar.gz
```

The third command mv renames the directory from mahout-distribution-0.9 to mahout:

```
sudo mv mahout-distribution-0.9 mahout
```

The last command chown changes the ownership of the file from the root user to the current user. The Linux command chown is used for changing the ownership of files and directories. The argument -R instructs the chown command to recursively change the ownership of subdirectories and $USER holds the value of the logged in user's username:

```
sudo chown -R $USER mahout
```

We need to update the .bashrc file to export the required variables and update the $PATH variable:

```
cd $HOME
vi .bashrc
```

At the end of the file, copy the following statements:

```
#Statements related to Mahout
export MAVEN_HOME=/usr/local/maven
export MAHOUT_HOME=/usr/local/mahout
PATH=$PATH:/bin:$MAVEN_HOME/bin:$MAHOUT_HOME/bin
###end of mahout statement
```

Exit from all existing terminals, start a new terminal, and enter the following command:

```
echo $PATH
```

Check whether the output has the path recently added to Maven and Mahout.

Type the following commands on the command line; both commands should be recognized:

```
mvn --version
mahout
```

Configuring Eclipse with the Maven plugin and Mahout

Download Eclipse from the Eclipse mirror mentioned on the home page. We have used Eclipse Kepler SR2 for this book. The downloaded archive should be in the Downloads folder of the user's home directory. Open a terminal and enter the following command:

```
cd /usr/local
sudo tar xzf $HOME/Downloads/eclipse-standard-kepler-SR2-linux-
gtk-x86_64.tar.gz
sudo chown -R $USER eclipse
```

Go into the Eclipse directory and open up the Eclipse GUI. We will now install the Maven plugin. Click on **Help** then **Eclipse Marketplace** and then in the search panel type m2e and search. Once the search results are displayed hit **Install** and follow the instructions. To complete the installation hit the **Next** button and press the **Accept** button whenever prompted. Once the installation is done, Eclipse will prompt for a restart. Hit OK and let Eclipse restart.

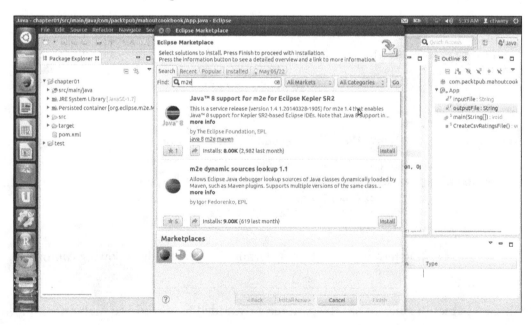

Now to add Mahout dependency to any Maven project we need, add the following dependency in the `pom.xml` file:

```
<dependency>
   <groupId>org.apache.mahout</groupId>
   <artifactId>mahout-core</artifactId>
   <version>0.9</version>
</dependency>
<dependency>
   <groupId>org.apache.mahout</groupId>
   <artifactId>mahout-examples</artifactId>
   <version>0.9</version>
</dependency>
<dependency>
   <groupId>org.apache.mahout</groupId>
   <artifactId>mahout-math</artifactId>
   <version>0.9</version>
</dependency>
```

Eclipse will download and add all the dependencies.

Now we should import the code repository of this book to Eclipse. Open Eclipse and follow the following sequence of steps. The `pom.xml` file has all the dependencies included in it and Eclipse will download and resolve the dependencies.

Go to **File** | **Import** | **Maven** | **Existing Maven Projects** | **Next** | Browse to the location of the source folder that comes with this book | **Finish**.

Downloading the example code

You can download the example code files from your account at http://www.packtpub.com for all the Packt Publishing books you have purchased. If you purchased this book elsewhere, you can visit http://www.packtpub.com/support and register to have the files e-mailed directly to you.

Mahout command line

Mahout provides an option for the command line execution of machine learning algorithms. Using the command line, an initial prototype of the model can be built quickly.

A few examples of command line are discussed. A great place to start is to go through Mahout's example scripts, the example scripts; are located under the Mahout home folder in the examples folder:

```
cd $MAHOUT_HOME
cd examples/bin
ls --ltr
```

The Mahout example scripts are as follows:

Open the file README.txt in vi editor and read the description of the scripts. We will be discussing them in the subsequent sections of this chapter:

```
vi README.txt
```

The description of the example script is as follows:

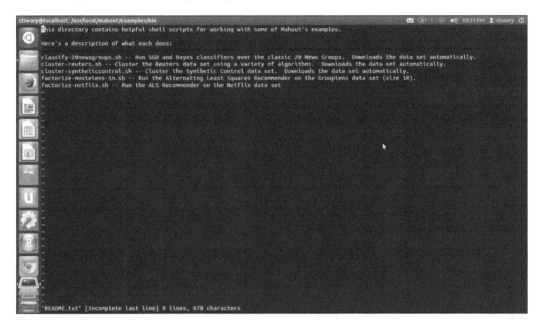

It is a good idea to try out a few command line Mahout algorithms before writing Mahout Java code. This way we can shortlist a few algorithms that might work on the given data and problem, and save a lot of time.

A clustering example

In this section, we will discuss the command line implementation of clustering in Mahout and use the example script as reference.

On the terminal please type:

```
vi cluster-reuters.sh
```

This script clusters the Reuters dataset using a variety of algorithms. It downloads the dataset automatically, parses and copies it to **HDFS** (**Hadoop Distributed File System**), and based upon user input, runs the corresponding clustering algorithm.

On the `vi` terminal type the command:

```
:set number
```

This will display the line numbers of the lines in the file. The algorithms implemented are `kmeans`, `fuzzykmeans`, `lda`, and `streamingkmeans`; line 42 of the code has a list of all algorithms implemented in the script:

```
algorithm=( kmeansfuzzykmeansldastreamingkmeans) #A list of all
algorithms implemented in the script
```

Input is taken from the user in line 51 by the `read` statement:

```
read -p "Enter your choice : " choice
```

Line 57 sets the `temp` working directory variable:

```
WORK_DIR=/tmp/mahout-work-${USER}
```

On line 79, the `curl` statement downloads the Reuters data to the working directory, first checking whether the file is already present in the working directory between lines 70 to 73:

```
curl http://kdd.ics.uci.edu/databases/reuters21578/reuters21578.tar.gz -o
${WORK_DIR}/reuters21578.tar.gz
```

From line 89, the Reuters `tar` is extracted to the `reuters-sgm` folder under the working directory:

```
tar xzf ${WORK_DIR}/reuters21578.tar.gz -C ${WORK_DIR}/reuters-sgm
```

Reuter's raw data file

Let's have a look at one of the `raw` files. Open the `reut2-000.sgm` file in a text editor such as `vi` or `gedit`.

The Reuter's `raw` file looks like this:

The Reuters data is distributed in 22 files, each of which contains 1,000 documents, except for the last (`reut2-021.sgm`), which contains 578 documents. The files are in the **SGML (standard generalized markup language)** format, which is similar to XML. The SGML file needs to be parsed.

On line 93, the Reuters data is parsed using Lucene. Lucene has built-in classes and functions to process different file formats. The logic of parsing the Reuters dataset is implemented in the `ExtractReuters` class. The SGML file is parsed and the text elements are extracted from it.

 Apache Lucene is a free/open source information retrieval software library.

We will use the `ExtractReuters` class to extract the `sgm` file to text format.

```
$MAHOUT org.apache.lucene.benchmark.utils.ExtractReuters ${WORK_DIR}/
reuters-sgm ${WORK_DIR}/reuters-out
```

Now let's look at the Reuters processed file. The following figure is a snapshot taken from the text file extracted from the sgm files we saw previously by the ExtractReuters class:

On lines 95 to 101, data is loaded from a local directory to HDFS, deleting the reuters-sgm and reuters-out folders if they already exist:

```
echo "Copying Reuters data to Hadoop"
$HADOOP dfs -rmr ${WORK_DIR}/reuters-sgm
$HADOOP dfs -rmr ${WORK_DIR}/reuters-out
$HADOOP dfs -put ${WORK_DIR}/reuters-sgm ${WORK_DIR}/reuters-sgm
$HADOOP dfs -put ${WORK_DIR}/reuters-out ${WORK_DIR}/reuters-out
```

On line 105, the files are converted into sequence files. Mahout works with sequence files.

 Sequence files are the standard input of Mahout machine learning algorithms.

```
$MAHOUT seqdirectory -i ${WORK_DIR}/reuters-out -o ${WORK_DIR}/reuters-out-seqdir -c UTF-8 -chunk 64 -xm sequential
```

On lines 109 to 111, the sequence file is converted to a vector representation. Text needs to be converted into a vector representation so that a machine learning algorithm can process it. We will talk about text vectorization in details in *Chapter 10, Case Study – Text Analytics*.

```
$MAHOUT seq2sparse -i ${WORK_DIR}/reuters-out-seqdir/
 -o ${WORK_DIR}/reuters-out-seqdir-sparse-kmeans --maxDFPercent 85 -
namedVector
```

From here on, we will only explain the k-means algorithm execution; we encourage you to read and understand the other three implementations too. A detailed discussion of clustering will be covered in *Chapter 7, Clustering with Mahout*.

Clustering is the process of partitioning a bunch of data points into related groups called clusters. K-means clustering partitions a dataset into a specified number of clusters by minimizing the distance between each data point and the center of the cluster using a distance metric. A distance metric is a way to define how far or near a data point is from another. K-means requires users to provide the number of clusters and optionally user-defined cluster centroids.

To better understand how data points are clustered together, please have a look at the sample figure displaying three clusters. Notice that the points that are nearby are grouped together into three distinct clusters. A few points don't belong to any clusters, those points represent outliers and should be removed prior to clustering.

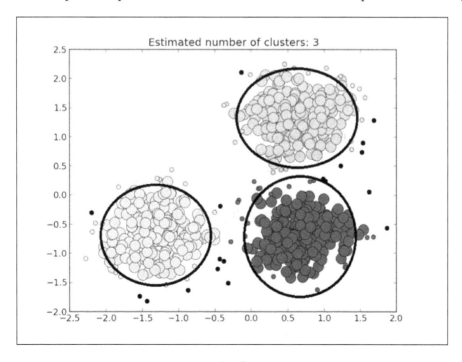

Here is an example of the command line for k-means clustering:

Parameter	Description
--input (-i)	This is the path to the job input directory.
--clusters (-c)	These are the input centroids and they must be a `SequenceFile` of type `Writable` or `Cluster/Canopy`. If k is also specified, then a random set of vectors will be selected and written out to this path first.
--output (-o)	This is the directory pathname for the output.
--distanceMeasure	This is the class name of `DistanceMeasure`; the default is `SquaredEuclidean`.
--convergenceDelta	This is the convergence delta value; the default is `0.5`.
--maxIter (-x)	This is the maximum number of iterations.
--maxRed (-r)	This is the number of reduce tasks; this defaults to `2`.
--k (-k)	This is the k in k-means. If specified, then a random selection of k vectors will be chosen as the `Centroid` and written to the cluster's input path.
--overwrite (-ow)	If this is present, overwrite the output directory before running the job.
--help (-h)	This prints out `Help`.
--clustering (-cl)	If this is present, run clustering after the iterations have taken place.

Lines 113 to 118 take the sparse matrix and runs the k-means clustering algorithm using the cosine distance metric. We pass -k the number of clusters as 20 and -x the maximum number of iterations as 10:

```
$MAHOUT kmeans \
-i ${WORK_DIR}/reuters-out-seqdir-sparse-kmeans/tfidf-vectors/ \
-c ${WORK_DIR}/reuters-kmeans-clusters \
-o ${WORK_DIR}/reuters-kmeans \
-dm org.apache.mahout.common.distance.CosineDistanceMeasure \
-x 10 -k 20 -ow --clustering \
```

Lines 120 to 125 take the cluster dump utility, read the clusters in sequence file format, and convert them to text files:

```
$MAHOUT clusterdump \
    -i ${WORK_DIR}/reuters-kmeans/clusters-*-final \
    -o ${WORK_DIR}/reuters-kmeans/clusterdump \
    -d ${WORK_DIR}/reuters-out-seqdir-sparse-kmeans/dictionary.file-0 \
```

```
    -dt sequencefile -b 100 -n 20 --evaluate -dm org.apache.mahout.
common.distance.CosineDistanceMeasure -sp 0 \
    --pointsDir ${WORK_DIR}/reuters-kmeans/clusteredPoints \
&& \
  cat ${WORK_DIR}/reuters-kmeans/clusterdump
```

The `clusterdump` utility outputs the center of each cluster and the top terms in the cluster. A sample of the output is shown here:

```
    Weight : [props - optional]:  Point:

VL-17939{n=1223 c=[0:0.039, 0.01:0.007, 0.025:0.008, 0.04:0.008, 0.05:0.014, 0.0625:0.016, 0.07:0.02
    Top Terms:
                pct                        =>    2.7694996027116003
                1                          =>      2.63786430390078
                4                          =>    2.1153221974485934
                8                          =>     2.053075326824422
                bond                       =>    1.9461722151724317
                mln                        =>    1.8959636700903892
                issue                      =>    1.8918351764476211
                lead                       =>    1.8233899489252272
                coupon                     =>    1.7956528815692891
                manager                    =>    1.7729487918189384
                2                          =>     1.719011329961232
                bank                       =>    1.6741793239496814
                priced                     =>    1.5499589047467035
                due                        =>     1.468868115644229
                said                       =>    1.4006727342223497
                issuing                    =>    1.278250590563795
                5                          =>    1.2619637134907582
                ltd                        =>    1.2222211218621042
                issues                     =>     1.20108258324574
                eurobond                   =>    1.1860761322745124
    Weight : [props - optional]:  Point:
```

A classification example

In this section, we will discuss the command line implementation of classification in Mahout and use the example script as a reference.

Classification is the task of identifying which set of predefined classes a data point belongs to. Classification involves training a model with a labeled (previously classified) dataset and then predicting new unlabeled data using that model. The common workflow for a classification problem is:

1. Data preparation
2. Train model
3. Test model
4. Performance measurement

Repeat steps until the desired performance is achieved, or the best possible solution is achieved or the project's time is up.

On the terminal, please type:

```
vi classify-20newsgroups.sh
```

On the vi terminal, type the following command to show the line numbers for lines in the script:

```
:set number
```

The algorithms implemented in the script are cnaivebayes, naivebayes, sgd, and a last option clean, which cleans up the work directory

Line 44 creates a working directory for the dataset and all input/output:

```
export WORK_DIR=/tmp/mahout-work-${USER}
```

Lines 64 to 74 download and extract the 20news-bydate.tar.gz file after making sure it is not already downloaded:

```
  if [ ! -e ${WORK_DIR}/20news-bayesinput ]; then
    if [ ! -e ${WORK_DIR}/20news-bydate ]; then
      if [ ! -f ${WORK_DIR}/20news-bydate.tar.gz ]; then
        echo "Downloading 20news-bydate"
        curl http://people.csail.mit.edu/jrennie/20Newsgroups/20news-
bydate.tar.gz -o ${WORK_DIR}/20news-bydate.tar.gz
      fi
      mkdir -p ${WORK_DIR}/20news-bydate
      echo "Extracting..."
      cd ${WORK_DIR}/20news-bydate && tar xzf ../20news-bydate.tar.gz &&
cd ..&&cd ..
    fi
  fi
```

The 20 newsgroup data has one message per file. Each file starts with header lines and has information about the sender, the length of the message, software used for sending the email and the subject. It is followed by the email body.

Lines 90 to 101 prepare the directory and copy the data to the Hadoop directory:

```
  echo "Preparing 20newsgroups data"
  rm -rf ${WORK_DIR}/20news-all
  mkdir ${WORK_DIR}/20news-all
  cp -R ${WORK_DIR}/20news-bydate/*/* ${WORK_DIR}/20news-all

  if [ "$HADOOP_HOME" != "" ] && [ "$MAHOUT_LOCAL" == "" ] ; then
    echo "Copying 20newsgroups data to HDFS"
```

```
    set +e
    $HADOOP dfs -rmr ${WORK_DIR}/20news-all
    set -e
    $HADOOP dfs -put ${WORK_DIR}/20news-all ${WORK_DIR}/20news-all
  fi
```

A snapshot of the raw `20newsgroups` data file is provided below.

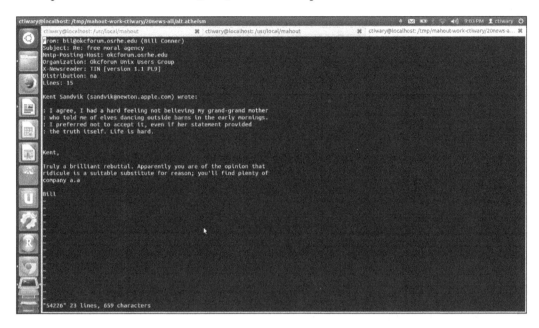

Lines 104 to 106 convert the full 20 newsgroups dataset into sequence files:

```
$ mahout seqdirectory  -i ${WORK_DIR}/20news-all -o ${WORK_DIR}/20news-
seq -ow
```

Lines 109 to 111 convert the sequence files to vectors calculating the term frequency and inverse document frequency. Term frequency and inverse document frequency are ways of representing text using numeric representation:

```
./bin/mahout seq2sparse \
-i ${WORK_DIR}/20news-seq \
-o ${WORK_DIR}/20news-vectors -lnorm -nv  -wt tfidf
```

Lines 114 to 118 split the preprocessed dataset into training and testing sets. The test set will be used to test the performance of the model trained using the training sets:

```
./bin/mahout split \
-i ${WORK_DIR}/20news-vectors/tfidf-vectors \
--trainingOutput ${WORK_DIR}/20news-train-vectors \
--testOutput ${WORK_DIR}/20news-test-vectors  \
--randomSelectionPct 40 --overwrite --sequenceFiles -xm sequential
```

Lines 120 to 125 train the classifier using the training sets:

```
./bin/mahout trainnb \
-i ${WORK_DIR}/20news-train-vectors -el \
-o ${WORK_DIR}/model \
-li ${WORK_DIR}/labelindex \
-ow $c
```

Lines 129 to 133 test the classifier using the test sets:

```
./bin/mahout testnb \
-i ${WORK_DIR}/20news-train-vectors\
-m ${WORK_DIR}/model \
-l ${WORK_DIR}/labelindex \
-ow -o ${WORK_DIR}/20news-testing $c
```

Mahout API – a Java program example

Though using Mahout from the command line is convenient, fast, and serves the purpose in many scenarios, learning the Mahout API is important too. The reason being, using the API gives you more flexibility in terms of creating your machine learning application, and not all algorithms can be easily called from the command line. Working with the Mahout API helps to understand the internals of a machine learning algorithm.

Mahout core JAR files have the implementation of the main machine learning classes and the Mahout examples JAR file has some example code and wrappers built around the Mahout core classes. It is worth spending time going through the documentation and getting an overall understanding. The documentation for the version you are using can be found in the Mahout installation directory.

The Mahout documentation directory looks like this:

We will now look at a Mahout code example. We will write a classification example in which we will train an algorithm to predict whether a client has subscribed to a term deposit. Classification refers to the process of labeling a particular instance or row to a particular predefined category, called a class label. The purpose of the following example is to give you a hang of the development using Mahout, Eclipse, and Maven.

The dataset

We will use the `bank-additional-full.csv` file present in the `learningApacheMahout/data/chapter4` directory as the input for our example. The data set has been taken from the data repository `http://mlr.cs.umass.edu/ml/datasets/Bank+Marketing` with the citation [Moro et al., 2014] S. Moro, P. Cortez and P. Rita. A Data-Driven Approach to Predict the Success of Bank Telemarketing. Decision Support Systems, Elsevier, 62:22-31, June 2014. First, let's have a look at the structure of the data and try to understand it. The following table shows various input variables along with their data types:

Column Name	Description	Variable Type
Age	Age of the client	Numeric
Job	Type of job, for example, entrepreneur, housemaid, or management	Categorical
Marital	Marital status	Categorical

Column Name	Description	Variable Type
Education	Education level	Categorical
Default	Has the client defaulted on credit?	Categorical
Housing	Does the client have housing loan?	Categorical
Loan	Does the client have personal loan?	Categorical
Contact	Contact communication type	Categorical
Month	Last contact month of year	Categorical
day_of_week	Last contact day of the week	Categorical
duration	Last contact duration, in seconds	Numeric
campaign	Number of contacts	Numeric
Pdays	Number of days that passed since last contact	Numeric
previous	Number of contacts performed before this campaign	Numeric
poutcome	outcome of the previous marketing campaign	Categorical
emp.var.rate	Employment variation rate - quarterly indicator	Numeric
cons.price.idx	Consumer price index - monthly indicator	Numeric
cons.conf.idx	Consumer confidence index - monthly indicator	Numeric
euribor3m	Euribor 3 month rate - daily indicator	Numeric
nr.employed	Number of employees - quarterly indicator	Numeric
Y	Has the client subscribed a term deposit	Categorical/ target

Based on many attributes of the customer, we try to predict the target variable y (has the client subscribed to a term deposit?), which has a set of two predefined values, *Yes* and *No*. We need to remove the header line to use the data.

We will use logistic regression to build the model; logistic regression is a statistical technique that computes the probability of an unclassified item belonging to a predefined class.

You might like to run the example with the code in the source code that ships with this book; I will explain the important steps in the following section. In Eclipse, open the code file OnlineLogisticRegressionTrain.java from the package chapter4. logistic.src, which is present in the directory learningApacheMahout/src/ main/java/chapter4/src/logistic in the code folder that comes with this book.

The first step is to identify the source and target folders:

```
String inputFile = "data/chapter4/train_data/input_bank_data.csv";
String outputFile = "data/chapter4/model";
```

Once we know where to get the data from, we need to tell the algorithm about how to interpret the data. We pass the column name and the corresponding column type; here, *n* denotes the numeric column and *w*, the categorical columns of the data:

```
List<String> predictorList =Arrays.asList("age","job","marital","educat
ion","default","housing","loan","contact","month","day_of_week","durati
on","campaign","pdays","previous","poutcome","emp.var.rate","cons.price.
idx","cons.conf.idx","euribor3m","nr.employed");

List<String> typeList = Arrays.asList("n","w","w","w","w","w","w","w","w"
,"w","n","n","n","n","w","n","n","n","n","n");
```

Set the classifier parameters. `LogisticModelParameters` is a wrapper class, in Mahout's example distribution, used to set the parameters for training logistic regression and to return the instance of a `CsvRecordFactory`:

```
LogisticModelParameters lmp = new LogisticModelParameters();
        lmp.setTargetVariable("y");
        lmp.setMaxTargetCategories(2);
        lmp.setNumFeatures(20);
        lmp.setUseBias(false);
        lmp.setTypeMap(predictorList,typeList);
        lmp.setLearningRate(0.5);
        int passes = 50;
```

We set the the target variable *y* to be used for training, the maximum number of target categories to be 2 (*Yes, No*), the number of features or columns in the data excluding the target variable (which is 20), and some other settings (which we will learn about later in this book). The variable passed has been given a value of 50, which means the maximum number of iteration over the data will be 50.

The `CsvRecordFactory` class returns an object to parse the CSV file based on the parameters passed. The `LogisticModelParameters` class takes care of passing the parameters to the constructor of `CsvRecordFactory`. We use the class `RandomAccessSparseVector` to encode the data into vectors and train the model using `lr.train(targetValue, input)`:

```
CsvRecordFactory csv = lmp.getCsvRecordFactory();
lr = lmp.createRegression();
for (int pass = 0; pass < passes; pass++) {
                BufferedReader in = new BufferedReader(new
FileReader(inputFile));


                csv.firstLine(in.readLine());
```

```
            String line = in.readLine();
            int lineCount = 2;
            while (line != null) {

            Vector input = new RandomAccessSparseVector(lmp.
getNumFeatures());
            int targetValue = csv.processLine(line, input);

            // update model
            lr.train(targetValue, input);
            k++;

            line = in.readLine();
            lineCount++;
        }
        in.close();
    }
```

The output after running the code would be an equation denoting the logistic regression. Excerpts of the equation are copied here:

```
y ~ -97.230*age + -12.713*campaign + . . .
```

You will learn about logistic regression, how to interpret the equation, and how to evaluate the results in detail in *Chapter 4, Classification with Mahout*.

Parallel versus in-memory execution mode

Mahout has both parallel and in-memory execution for many machine learning algorithms. In-memory execution can be used when the data size is smaller or to try out different algorithms quickly without installing Hadoop. In-memory execution is restricted to one machine whereas the parallel are designed to run on different machines. The parallel execution is implemented over Hadoop using the MapReduce paradigm, and for parallel execution; we call the code via the driver class to run the Hadoop MapReduce job. Let's see which algorithms have single machine and parallel execution. We have grouped the algorithms according to the paradigm such as collaborative filtering, classification, and so on. The first column of the table is the name of the column, the second column indicates whether the algorithm has a single machine implementation, and the third column indicates whether the algorithm has a parallel execution implementation.

The collaborative filtering table is as follows:

Algorithm	Single machine	Parallel
User-based collaborative filtering	Y	N
Item-based collaborative filtering	Y	Y
Matrix factorization with alternating least squares	Y	Y
Matrix factorization with alternating least squares on implicit feedback	Y	Y
Weighted matrix factorization	Y	N

The classification table is as follows:

Algorithm	Single machine	Parallel
Logistic regression	Y	N
Naïve Bayes/Complementary naïve Bayes	N	Y
Random forest	N	Y
Hidden Markov models	Y	N
Multilayer perceptron	Y	N

The clustering table is as follows:

Algorithm	Single machine	Parallel
Canopy clustering	Y	Y
k-means clustering	Y	Y
Fuzzy k-means	Y	Y
Streaming k-means	Y	Y
Spectral clustering	N	Y

The dimensionality reduction table is as follows:

Algorithm	Single machine	Parallel
Singular value decomposition	Y	N
Lanczos algorithm	Y	Y
Stochastic SVD	Y	Y
Principal component analysis	Y	Y

The topic models table is as follows:

Algorithm	Single machine	Parallel
Latent Dirichlet allocation	Y	Y

The miscellaneous table is as follows:

Algorithm	Single machine	Parallel
Frequent pattern mining	N	Y
RowSimilarityJob	N	Y
ConcatMatrices	N	Y
Collocations	N	Y

Summary

In this chapter, we discussed the guiding principle of Mahout and tried out some examples to get a hands-on feel of Mahout. We discussed why, when, and how to use Mahout and walked through the installation steps of the required tools and software. We then learned how to use Mahout from the command line and from the code, and finally concluded with a comparison between the parallel and the single-machine execution of Mahout.

This is the beginning of what will hopefully be an exciting journey. In the forthcoming chapters, we will discuss a lot of practical applications for Mahout. In the next chapter, we will discuss the core concepts of machine learning. A clear understanding of the concepts of different machine learning algorithms is of paramount importance for a successful career in data analytics.

2
Core Concepts in Machine Learning

The purpose of this chapter is to understand the core concepts of machine learning. We will focus on understanding the steps involved in, resolving different types of problems and application areas in machine learning. In particular we will cover the following topics:

- Supervised learning
- Unsupervised learning
- The recommender system
- Model efficacy

A wide range of software applications today try to replace or augment human judgment. Artificial Intelligence is a branch of computer science that has long been trying to replicate human intelligence. A subset of AI, referred to as machine learning, tries to build intelligent systems by using the data. For example, a machine learning system can learn to classify different species of flowers or group-related news items together to form categories such as news, sports, politics, and so on, and for each of these tasks, the system will learn using data. For each of the tasks, the corresponding algorithm would look at the data and try to learn from it. In the next few sections, you will learn about the major concepts and paradigms related to machine learning.

Supervised learning

Supervised learning deals with training algorithms with labeled data, inputs for which the outcome or target variables are known, and then predicting the outcome/target with the trained model for unseen future data. For example, historical e-mail data will have individual e-mails marked as ham or spam; this data is then used for training a model that can predict future e-mails as ham or spam. Supervised learning problems can be broadly divided into two major areas, **classification** and **regression**.

Classification deals with predicting categorical variables or classes; for example, whether an e-mail is ham or spam or whether a customer is going to renew a subscription or not, for example a postpaid telecom subscription. This target variable is discrete, and has a predefined set of values.

Regression deals with a target variable, which is continuous. For example, when we need to predict house prices, the target variable price is continuous and doesn't have a predefined set of values.

In order to solve a given problem of supervised learning, one has to perform the following steps.

Determine the objective

The first major step is to define the objective of the problem. Identification of class labels, what is the acceptable prediction accuracy, how far in the future is prediction required, is insight more important or is accuracy of classification the driving factor, these are the typical objectives that need to be defined. For example, for a churn classification problem, we could define the objective as identifying customers who are most likely to churn within three months. In this case, the class label from the historical data would be whether a customer has churned or not, with insights into the reasons for the churn and a prediction of churn at least three months in advance.

Decide the training data

After the objective of the problem has been defined, the next step is to decide what training data should be used. The training data is directly guided by the objective of the problem to be solved. For example, in the case of an e-mail classification system, it would be historical e-mails, related metadata, and a label marking each e-mail as spam or ham. For the problem of churn analysis, different data points collected about a customer such as product usage, support case, and so on, and a target label for whether a customer has churned or is active, together form the training data.

Churn Analytics is a major problem area for a lot of businesses domains such as BFSI, telecommunications, and SaaS. Churn is applicable in circumstances where there is a concept of term-bound subscription. For example, postpaid telecom customers subscribe for a monthly term and can choose to renew or cancel their subscription. A customer who cancels this subscription is called a churned customer.

Create and clean the training set

The next step in a machine learning project is to gather and clean the dataset. The sample dataset needs to be representative of the real-world data, though all available data should be used, if possible. For example, if we assume that 10 percent of e-mails are spam, then our sample should ideally start with 10 percent spam and 90 percent ham. Thus, a set of input rows and corresponding target labels are gathered from data sources such as warehouses, or logs, or operational database systems. If possible, it is advisable to use all the data available rather than sampling the data. Cleaning data for data quality purposes forms part of this process. For example, training data inclusion criteria should also be explored in this step. An example of this in the case of customer analytics is to decide the minimum age or type of customers to use in the training set, for example including customers aged at least six months.

Feature extraction

Determine and create the feature set from the training data. Features or predictor variables are representations of the training data that is used as input to a model. Feature extraction involves transforming and summarizing that data. The performance of the learned model depends strongly on its input feature set. This process is primarily called feature extraction and requires good understanding of data and is aided by domain expertise. For example, for churn analytics, we use demography information from the CRM, product adoption (phone usage in case of telecom), age of customer, and payment and subscription history as the features for the model. The number of features extracted should neither be too large nor too small; feature extraction is more art than science and, optimum feature representation can be achieved after some iterations. Typically, the dataset is constructed such that each row corresponds to one variable outcome. For example, in the churn problem, the training dataset would be constructed so that every row represents a customer.

Train the models

We need to try out different supervised learning algorithms. This step is called training the model and is an iterative process where you might try building different training samples and try out different combinations of features. For example, we may choose to use support vector machines or decision trees depending upon the objective of the study, the type of problem, and the available data. Machine learning algorithms can be bucketed into groups based on the ability of a user to interpret how the predictions were arrived at. If the model can be interpreted easily, then it is called a white box, for example decision tree and logistic regression, and if the model cannot be interpreted easily, they belong to the black box models, for example **support vector machine** (**SVM**). If the objective is to gain insight, a white box model such as decision tree or logistic regression can be used, and if robust prediction is the criteria, then algorithms such as neural networks or support vector machines can be used.

While training a model, there are a few techniques that we should keep in mind, like bagging and boosting.

Bagging

Bootstrap aggregating, which is also known as bagging, is a technique where the data is sampled from the original dataset N times to make N new datasets. The new datasets are of the same size as the original dataset and are built by randomly selecting an example from the *original with replacement*. By with replacement we mean that we can select the same example more than once. This property allows us to have values in the new dataset that are repeated, and some values from the original won't be present in the new set. Bagging helps in reducing the variance of a model and can be used to train different models using the same datasets. The final conclusion is arrived at after considering the output of each model.

For example, let's assume our data is *a, b, c, d, e, f, g,* and *h*. By sampling our data five times, we can create five different samples as follows:

- Sample 1: *a, b, c, c, e, f, g, h*
- Sample 2: *a, b, c, d, d, f, g, h*
- Sample 3: *a, b, c, c, e, f, h, h*
- Sample 4: *a, b, c, e, e, f, g, h*
- Sample 5: *a, b, b, e, e, f, g, h*

As we sample with replacement, we get the same examples more than once. Now we can train five different models using the five sample datasets. Now, for the prediction; as each model will provide the output, let's assume classes are *yes* and *no*, and the final outcome would be the class with maximum votes. If three models say *yes* and two *no*, then the final prediction would be class *yes*.

Boosting

Boosting is a technique of ensemble of models and in approach is similar to bagging. In boosting and bagging, we always use the same type of classifier but in boosting, the different classifiers are trained sequentially as against the parallel training in bagging. Each new classifier is trained based on the performance of those already trained and gives greater weight to examples that were misclassified by the previous classifier. Boosting focuses new classifiers to be trained on previously misclassified data.

Boosting also differs from bagging in its approach of calculating the final prediction. The output is calculated from a weighted sum of all classifiers output, as opposed to the method of equal weights used in bagging. The weights assigned to the classifier output in boosting are based on the performance of the classifier in the previous iteration.

Validation

After collecting the training set and extracting the features, you need to train the model and validate it on unseen samples. There are many approaches for creating the unseen sample called the validation set. We will be discussing a couple of them shortly.

Holdout-set validation

One approach to creating the validation set is to divide the feature set into train and test samples. We use the train set to train the model and test set to validate it. The actual percentage split varies from case to case but commonly it is split at 70 percent train and 30 percent test. It is also not uncommon to create three sets, train, test and validation set. Train and test set is created from data out of all considered time periods but the validation set is created from the most recent data.

K-fold cross validation

Another approach is to divide the data into *k* equal size folds or parts and then use *k-1* of them for training and one for testing. The process is repeated *k* times so that each set is used as a validation set once and the metrics are collected over all the runs. The general standard is to use *k* as *10*, which is called 10-fold cross-validation.

Evaluation

The objective of evaluation is to test the generalization of a classifier. By generalization, we mean how good the model performs on future data. Ideally, evaluation should be done on an unseen sample, separate to the validation sample or by cross-validation. There are standard metrics to evaluate a classifier against. We will discuss them in the model efficacy section. There are a few things to consider while training a classifier that we should keep in mind. We will discuss those in this section.

Bias-variance trade-off

The first aspect to keep in mind is the trade-off between **bias** and **variance**.

To understand the meaning of bias and variance, let's assume that we have several different, but equally good, training datasets for a specific supervised learning problem. We train different models using the same technique; for example, build different decision trees using the different training datasets available.

Bias measures how far off in general a model's predictions are from the correct value. Bias can be measured as the average difference between a predicted output and its actual value. A learning algorithm is biased for a particular input X if, when trained on different training sets, it is incorrect when predicting the correct output for X.

Variance is how greatly the predictions for a given point vary between different realizations of the model. A learning algorithm is said to have a high variance for a particular input X if it predicts different output values for X when trained on different subsets of the same training sets.

Generally, there is always a trade-off between bias and variance. A learning algorithm with low bias needs to be flexible so that it can fit the data well. But if the learning algorithm is too flexible, it will fit each training dataset differently, and hence will have high variance. A key aspect of many supervised learning methods is that they are able to adjust this trade-off between bias and variance. The plot on the top left is the scatter plot of the original data. The plot on the top right is a fit with high bias; the error in prediction in this case will be high. The bottom left image is a fit with high variance; the model is very flexible, and error on the training set is low but the prediction on unseen data will have a much higher degree of error as compared to the training set. The bottom right plot is an optimum fit with a good trade-off of bias and variance. The model explains the data well and will perform in a similar way for unseen data too.

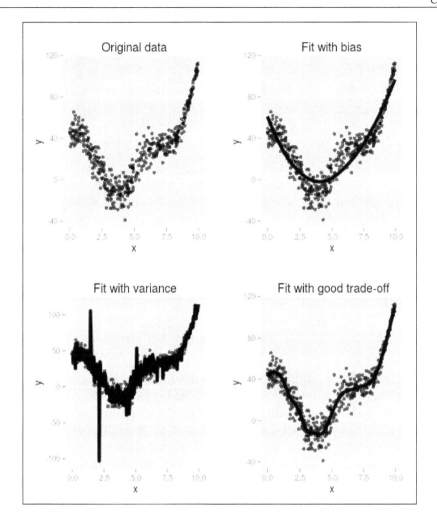

If the bias-variance trade-off is not optimized, it leads to problems of under-fitting and over-fitting. The plot shows a visual representation of the bias-variance trade-off.

Over-fitting occurs when an estimator is too flexible and tries to fit the data too closely. High variance and low bias leads to over-fitting of data.

Under-fitting occurs when a model is not flexible enough to capture the underlying trends in the observed data. Low variance and high bias leads to under-fitting of data.

Function complexity and amount of training data

The second aspect to consider is the amount of training data needed to train the model and learn the task at hand. The amount of data required is proportional to the complexity of the data, the learning algorithm and the learning task at hand. For example, if the features in the data have low interaction and have lower dimensionality, a decent model can be trained even with a small dataset. In this case, a learning algorithm with high bias and low variance is better suited.

But if the learning task at hand is complex, has higher dimensionality and with higher degree of interaction, then a larger dataset is required. In this case, a learning algorithm with low bias and high variance is better suited. It is difficult to actually determine the amount of data needed, but the complexity of the task provides some indications.

Dimensionality of the input space

A third aspect to consider is the dimensionality of the input space. By dimensionality, we mean the number of features the training set has. If the input feature set has a very high number of features, any machine learning algorithm will require a huge amount of data to build a good model.

In practice, it is advisable to remove any extra dimensionality before training the model; this is likely to improve the accuracy of the learned function. Techniques like feature selection and dimensionality reduction can be used for this. We will discuss in details the problems of higher dimensionality and a few of the techniques for dimensionality reduction in *Chapter 3, Feature Engineering*.

Noise in data

The fourth issue is noise. Noise refers to inaccuracies in data due to various issues. Noise can be present either in the predictor variables, or in the target variable. Both lead to model inaccuracies and reduce the generalization of the model.

In practice, there are several approaches to alleviate noise in the data; first would be to identify and then remove the noisy training examples prior to training the supervised learning algorithm, and second would be to have an early stopping criteria to prevent over-fitting.

Unsupervised learning

Unsupervised learning deals with unlabeled data. The objective is to observe structure in data and find patterns. Tasks like cluster analysis, association rule mining, outlier detection, dimensionality reduction, and so on can be modeled as unsupervised learning problems. As the tasks involved in unsupervised learning vary vastly, there is no single process outline that we can follow. We will follow the process of some of the most common unsupervised learning problems.

Cluster analysis

Cluster analysis is a subset of unsupervised learning that aims to create groups of similar items from a set of items. Real life examples could be clustering movies according to various attributes like genre, length, ratings, and so on. Cluster analysis helps us identify interesting groups of objects that we are interested in. It could be items we encounter in day-to-day life such as movies, songs according to taste, or interests of users in terms of their demography or purchasing patterns. Let's consider a small example so you understand what we mean by interesting groups and understand the power of clustering. We will use the Iris dataset, which is a standard dataset used for academic research and it contains five variables: sepal length, sepal width, petal length, petal width, and species with 150 observations. The first plot we see shows petal length against petal width. Each color represents a different species. The second plot is the groups identified by clustering the data.

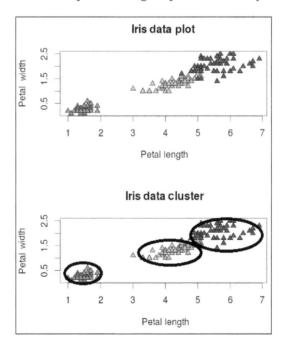

Looking at the plot, we can see that the plot of petal length against petal width clearly separates the species of the Iris flower and in the process, it clusters the group's flowers of the same species together. Cluster analysis can be used to identify interesting patterns in data.

The process of clustering involves these four steps. We will discuss each of them in the section ahead.

- Objective
- Feature representation
- Algorithm for clustering
- A stopping criteria

Objective

What do we want to cluster? This is an important question. Let's assume we have a large customer base for some kind of an e-commerce site and we want to group them together. How do we want to group them? Do we want to group our users according to their demography, such as age, location, income, and so on or are we interested in grouping them together? A clear objective is a good start, though it is not uncommon to start without an objective and see what can be done with the available data.

Feature representation

As with any machine learning task, feature representation is important for cluster analysis too. Creating derived features, summarizing data, and converting categorical variables to continuous variables are some of the common tasks. The feature representation needs to represent the objective of clustering. For example, if the objective is to cluster users based upon purchasing behavior, then features should be derived from purchase transaction and user demography information. If the objective is to cluster documents, then features should be extracted from the text of the document.

Feature normalization

To compare the feature vectors, we need to normalize them. Normalization could be across rows or across columns. In most cases, both are normalized.

Row normalization

The objective of normalizing rows is to make the objects to be clustered, comparable. Let's assume we are clustering organizations based upon their e-mailing behavior. Now organizations are very large and very small, but the objective is to capture the e-mailing behavior, irrespective of size of the organization. In this scenario, we need to figure out a way to normalize rows representing each organization, so that they can be compared. In this case, dividing by user count in each respective organization could give us a good feature representation. Row normalization is mostly driven by the business domain and requires domain expertise.

Column normalization

The range of data across columns varies across datasets. The unit could be different or the range of columns could be different, or both. There are many ways of normalizing data. Which technique to use varies from case to case and depends upon the objective. A few of them are discussed here.

Rescaling

The simplest method is to rescale the range of features so that the features have the same range. The aim of rescaling is to scale the features to the range in [0, 1] or [-1, 1], and the formula for the same is:

$$x' = \frac{x - \min(x)}{\max(x) - \min(x)}$$

Here x is the original value and x', the rescaled valued.

Standardization

Feature standardization transforms the values of each feature in the data to have zero-mean and unit-variance. To standardize features, we first calculate the mean and standard deviation for each feature and then subtract by the corresponding mean. Then, we divide the mean subtracted values of each feature by its standard deviation: $Xs = (X - mean(X)) / standard\ deviation(X)$.

A notion of similarity and dissimilarity

Once we have the objective defined, it leads to the idea of similarity and dissimilarity of object or data points. Since we need to group things together based on similarity, we need a way to measure similarity. Likewise to keep dissimilar things apart, we need a notion of dissimilarity. This idea is represented in machine learning by the idea of a distance measure. Distance measure, as the name suggests, is used to measure the distance between two objects or data points.

Euclidean distance measure

Euclidean distance measure is the most commonly used and intuitive distance measure:

$$d(p,q) = \sqrt{(p_1 - q_1)^2 + (p_2 - q_2)^2 + \ldots + (p_i - q_i)^2 + \ldots + (p_n - q_n)^2}$$

Squared Euclidean distance measure

The standard Euclidean distance, when squared, places progressively greater weight on objects that are farther apart as compared to the nearer objects. The equation to calculate squared Euclidean measure is shown here:

$$d^2(p,q) = (p_1 - q_1)^2 + (p_2 - q_2)^2 + \ldots + (p_i - q_i)^2 + \ldots + (p_n - q_n)^2$$

Manhattan distance measure

Manhattan distance measure is defined as the sum of the absolute difference of the coordinates of two points. The distance between two points measured along axes at right angles. In a plane with *p1* at *(x1, y1)* and *p2* at *(x2, y2)*, it is $|x1 - x2| + |y1 - y2|$:

$$d_1(\mathbf{p},\mathbf{q}) = \|\mathbf{p} - \mathbf{q}\|_1 = \sum_{i=1}^{n} |p_i - q_i|$$

Cosine distance measure is used when we have to measure the distance between two vectors without accounting for their magnitude. It measures the angle between the vectors and the intuition is that if the angle is small, then the vectors are pointing in the same direction and both are similar. The cosine of angle is close to 1 when the angle is small and decreases to -1 when the angle is largest. The cosine distance equation subtracts the cosine value from 1 so as the angle between the vectors grow, the distance becomes larger. The range of cosine distance is 0 to 2.

$$d = 1 - \frac{(a_1 b_1 + a_2 b_2 + \ldots + a_n b_n)}{\left(\sqrt{(a_1^2 + a_2^2 + \ldots + a_n^2)}\sqrt{(b_1^2 + b_2^2 + \ldots + b_n^2)}\right)}$$

Tanimoto distance measure

The Tanimoto distance measure, like the cosine distance measure, measures the angle between two points, as well as the relative distance between the points:

$$d = 1 - \frac{\left(a_1 b_1 + a_2 b_2 + \ldots + a_n b_n\right)}{\left(\sqrt{\left(a_1^2 + a_2^2 + \ldots + a_n^2\right)}\sqrt{\left(b_1^2 + b_2^2 + \ldots + b_n^2\right)}\right) - \left(a_1 b_1 + a_2 b_2 + \ldots + a_n b_n\right)}$$

Apart from the standard distance measure, we can also define our own distance measure. Custom distance measure can be explored when existing ones are not able to measure the similarity between items.

Algorithm for clustering

The type of clustering algorithm to be used is driven by the objective of the problem at hand. There are several options and the predominant ones are density-based clustering, distance-based clustering, distribution-based clustering, and hierarchical clustering. The choice of algorithm to be used depends upon the objective of the problem.

A stopping criteria

We need to know when to stop the clustering process. The stopping criteria could be decided in different ways: one way is when the cluster centroids don't move beyond a certain margin after multiple iterations, a second way is when the density of the clusters have stabilized, and third way could be based upon the number of iterations, for example stopping the algorithm after 100 iterations. The stopping criteria depends upon the algorithm used, the goal being to stop when we have good enough clusters.

Frequent pattern mining

Frequent pattern mining is a method to discover interesting relationships between variables in large databases. It is used to identify strong rules discovered in databases using different measures of interestingness; the measures will be discussed later on.

For example, the association rule {onions, potatoes]-+{burger} that can be discovered after mining the sales data of a store tells us that if a customer buys onions and potatoes together, he or she is likely to buy a burger. This information can be used to make decisions about promotional pricing or placements etc.

Measures for identifying interesting rules

The rules that are discovered in a database should be filtered by some criteria of interest, otherwise we will be flooded by a large number of insignificant rules. There are a few ways of defining the degree of interest and we will use a table to explain them:

Transaction	Product1	Product2	Product3	Product4
1	1	1	0	0
2	0	0	1	0
3	0	0	0	1
4	1	1	1	0
5	0	1	0	0

Support

The support *supp(x)* of an itemset X is defined as the proportion of transactions in the dataset, which contain the itemset. In the example database, the itemset {Product1, Product2, Product3} has a support of 2/5=0.4 since it occurs in 40 percent of all transactions (2 out of 5 transactions).

Confidence

The confidence of a rule is defined as $conf(x \rightarrow y) = supp(x \cup y) / supp(x)$. For example, the rule {Product3, Product2} $\rightarrow$ {Product1} has a confidence of 0.4/0.4=1.0 in the database, which means that 100 percent of the transactions containing Product3 and Product2 also contain Proudct1. Here sup(x U y) means support for occurrences of transactions where itemsets X and Y both appear.

Lift

The lift of a rule is defined as $lift(X \rightarrow Y) = supp(X \cup Y) / (supp(X) * supp(Y))$ or the ratio of the observed support to that expected if X and Y were independent. The rule {Product1, Product2} $\rightarrow$ {Product3} has a lift of 0.4/ (0.4 * 0.6) = 1.66.

Conviction

The conviction of a rule is defined as $conv(X \rightarrow Y) = (1 - supp(Y)) / (1 - conf(X \rightarrow Y))$. The rule {Product1, Product2} $\rightarrow$ {Product3} has a conviction of (1- 0.4)/ (1- 0.66) = 1.76, and it can be interpreted as the ratio of the expected frequency that X occurs without Y (that is to say, the frequency that the rule makes an incorrect prediction) if X and Y were independently divided by the observed frequency of incorrect predictions.

In this example, the conviction value of 1.2 shows that the rule {Product1, Product2} → { Product3} would be incorrect 20 percent more often (1.2 times as often) if the association between X and Y was a purely random chance.

Things to consider

For an association rule mining project to be successful, we need to consider a couple of things, which are discussed here.

Actionable rules

While filtering the association rules, focus should be on looking at actionable rules. Many a time, the algorithm will churn out simple rules such {Car} → {Car Insurance}, which though true, are as simple as a person buying a car is bound to buy car insurance. Similarly, we could get inexplicable rules, which might provide some insight, but are not very actionable.

What association to look for

Many rule mining implementations allow you to define the left or the right-hand side of the association to look for. Even if the particular implementation you are working on doesn't have that capability, you can always post-process the rules. This approach is particularly helpful when the data is very large and generates a lot of rules. The associations to look for could be defined in a discussion with the business users; for example, are they aware of the products that loyal customers buy and do they want to push some more related products to them? Or are they interested in identifying products that are not doing well and they want to replace it with some other products to push sales? In the former case, the known items would be on the right-hand side of the association and you could look at the left-hand side of the rules for insight; in the latter case, the product would be on the right-hand side and you could look at the left-hand side to find products to club together.

Recommender system

There is a lot of interest in recommending items to a user. Suppose a user goes to an e-commerce site, what should be recommended to the user? Items might be recommended based upon what a user previously liked, bought, or what their friends liked. Recommenders deal with discovering new items for which a user could have a higher preference.

Recommendations are computed using two major paradigms, collaborative and content based filtering. Collaborative filtering works on recommendations based upon user's past behaviour and behaviour of user's similar to the current user. Items based upon other similar items purchased are also taken into consideration. Content based filtering uses the characteristic of the item to be recommended to produce the recommendations. Let's assume that we need to recommend books. Collaborative filtering approach will recommend books based upon purchase history of similar users and similar books. Content based recommenders will take into account attributes about the book, like genre, length of book, author etc. These approaches are often combined to build a hybrid recommendation system.

Collaborative filtering

The first approach to a recommendation system that we will discuss is collaborative filtering. This approach is based on collecting and analyzing large amount of data based on the user's behavior, preferences, and activities such as browsing history, purchase history, and so on. The recommendations are generated for items that a user has not yet disclosed any preference, based upon similar users or similar items. A key point to note is that collaborative filtering doesn't take into account the attributes or characteristics of the item itself. We don't need to know anything about a book to recommend it.

The data points that are generally considered are as follows:

- History of the user's preference of items on a predefined scale, for example zero to five
- History of the user's searches and browsing history
- Items that the user has liked
- Items bought by the user over a period of time
- Information from the user's social network to discover similarity in likes and dislikes

There are a few common issues to keep in mind while creating a recommender system, they are as follows.

Cold start

Collaborative filtering often requires a large amount of existing data on a user, in order to make accurate recommendations. While designing a new system, we won't have data for user item interactions.

Scalability

Collaborative filtering algorithms normally need to analyze millions of records of different users and product. Scaling a recommender system to handle large volumes of data is a big challenge.

Sparsity

Sparse data, irrespective of the learning problem and algorithm, is always hard to model. The recommender system generally builds recommendations around a large number of items, whereas user activity typically is concentrated around a smaller subset of the items. For example, an e-commerce site sells a large number of items but the users would have provided preferences for a very small number of items. Addressing this scenario is not simple.

Content-based filtering

An alternative to collaborative filtering is content-based filtering, also called cognitive filtering. In contrast to collaborative filtering, content-based filtering depends on the understanding of the items to be recommended. Attributes are derived from the items that recommend the described items. A user profile is built that describes the interests of a user and recommendations are provided based on matching user and item descriptions. For example, if a user expresses an interest in action-based movies, then highly rated movies of the action genre could be recommended. We will be focusing on collaborative filtering in this book and content-based filtering will not be covered hereafter.

Model efficacy

The main goal of model building in machine learning is generalization, which is how well the model will perform its intended objective. Generalization means how the model would perform on new unseen data, typically data in production. To estimate the generalization of a model, we need to test its performance based on unseen data. The mechanism to do it varies, depending upon the task at hand.

Classification

In this section, we will discuss the common ways to evaluate the efficacy of a classification model.

Confusion matrix

One of the most common and basic ways of evaluating a model's performance is by creating a confusion matrix and computing various metrics such as accuracy, precision, recall, and so on. We will start with an example for two class classifiers to understand the concepts, and then extend it to problems involving more than two classes.

The confusion matrix is as follows:

Classifier		Predicted	
		Negative	Positive
	Negative	A	B
Actual	Positive	C	D

We label one class as positive and the other as negative. To illustrate some specific problems with an unbalanced dataset, we will consider examples with unbalanced class labels, where negative is ham and positive is spam.

The entries in the confusion matrix have the following meaning in the context of our study:

- A is the number of correct predictions that an instance is negative, where ham is predicted as ham.

- B is the number of incorrect predictions that an instance is positive, where ham is predicted as spam.

- C is the number of incorrect predictions that an instance is negative, where spam is predicted as ham.

- D is the number of correct predictions that an instance is positive, where spam is predicted as spam.

The performance metric derived from the confusion matrix is as follows:

- The accuracy (AC) is the proportion of the total number of predictions that were correct. It is determined using the equation:

$$AC = \frac{a+d}{a+b+c+d}$$

- The recall or true positive rate (TP) is the proportion of positive cases that were correctly identified, as calculated using the equation:

$$TP = \frac{d}{c+d}$$

- The false positive rate (FP) is the proportion of negative cases that were incorrectly classified as positive, as calculated using the equation:

$$FP = \frac{b}{a+b}$$

- The true negative rate (TN) is defined as the proportion of negatives cases that were classified correctly, as calculated using the equation:

$$TN = \frac{a}{a+b}$$

- The false negative rate (FN) is the proportion of positive cases that were incorrectly classified as negative, as calculated using the equation:

$$FN = \frac{c}{c+d}$$

- Finally, precision (P) is the proportion of the predicted positive cases that were correct, as calculated using the equation:

$$P = \frac{d}{b+d}$$

Another way of measuring a model's accuracy is to compute the **F-score**. The balanced F-score is the harmonic mean of precision and recall:

$$F_1 = 2 \cdot \frac{precision \cdot recall}{precision + recall}$$

For unbalanced class problems, where the number of one class is much greater than the other class, accuracy is not an adequate performance, particularly in cases where the minority class is of greater interest. For example let's suppose that there are 100 cases, 90 of which are negative cases and the number of positive cases are 10; if the system classifies them all as negative, the accuracy would be 90 percent, even though the classifier predicted all positive cases as wrong. In this scenario, we could use the general formula, as follows:

$$F_\beta = \left(1 + \beta^2\right) \cdot \frac{precision \cdot recall}{\left(\beta^2 \cdot precision\right) + recall}$$

β has a value from *0* to *infinity* and is used to control the weight assigned to TP and P. Typically, we can use the ratio of positive to negative cases as the value of β.

ROC curve and AUC

The ROC curve is an alternative way to evaluate the performance of classifiers. The ROC curve plots the false positive rate against the true positive rate. Typically, the false positive rate is plotted on the *x axis* and true positive rate is plotted on the *y axis*. The point (0, 1) represents the perfect classifier as the false positive rate is zero and true positive rate is 1. A similar deduction can be derived for (0,0), which denotes all cases as negative (1,0) and (1,1).

Features of ROC graphs

The features of the ROC graph are as follows:

- The ROC curve is independent of the class distribution of the data or the relative error costs of the classes

- The ROC graph represents all the information that can be derived from the confusion matrix and additionally, provides a visual representation of the performance of a classifier

- ROC curves provide a visual tool for examining the trade-off between the ability of a classifier to correctly identify positive cases and the number of negative cases that are incorrectly classified

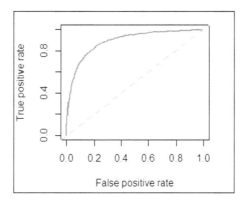

The red line plots the ROC curve.

Evaluating classifier using the ROC curve

Once we have built the ROC curve, there are a few standard ways to summarize a model performance from it.

Area-based accuracy measure

The area under the ROC curve, commonly known as AUC, can be used to estimate the performance of a model. AUC ranges between zero and one. The higher the value, the better the performance of a classifier. Generally, an AUC greater than eight is considered excellent and values between six and eight are considered good, but the thresholds should depend upon the task at hand. One point to note about AUC is that it is very important to look at the ROC curve itself, as two very different curves can have a similar AUC. AUC gives a good representative number for a model's performance but cannot replace the value of actually visualizing it on an ROC curve.

Euclidian distance comparison

As noted earlier, there could be scenarios where the cost of misclassification is not equal for each class and you learned how to address those scenarios using the F-measure. We could do the same using the ROC curve by measuring the Euclidean distance between the perfect classifier (0,1) and the current classifier. We include the weight factor W as having a range between zero and one and assign the weights W to the true positive and 1 - W to the false positive rate. This gives us the following formula:

$$AC_d = 1 - \sqrt{W * (1 - TP)^2 + (1 - W) * FP^2}$$

The range of value generated is 0 to square root of 2. The perfect classifier gets a score of 0 and a classifier which is always wrong gets a value of square root of zero.

Regression

In this section, we will discuss the common ways to evaluate the efficacy of a regression model.

Mean absolute error

Mean absolute error is defined as the mean of the magnitude of difference between the actual and the predicted values. The mean absolute error has the same unit as the original data, and it can only be compared between models whose errors are measured in the same units. During the calculation of absolute mean value, we don't consider the +- sign of the values

$$MAE = \frac{\sum_{i=1}^{n} |p_i - a_i|}{n}$$

Here p is the predicted value, a the actual value, and n the number of samples.

An alternative is a relative absolute error, which can be compared between models whose errors are measured in the different units. It is defined as the ratio of mean absolute error to the mean value of the measured quantity.

$$RAE = \frac{\sum_{i=1}^{n} |p_i - a_i|}{\sum_{i=1}^{n} |\bar{a} - a_i|}$$

Root mean squared error

RMSE is a popular formula used to measure the error rate of a regression model. However, it can only be compared between models whose errors are measured in the same units.

$$RMSE = \sqrt{\frac{\sum_{i=1}^{n}(p_i - a_i)^2}{n}}$$

Here p is the predicted value, a the actual value and n the number of samples. An alternative is to use **relative squared error** (**RSE**). The relative squared error can be compared between models whose errors are measured in the different units.

$$RSE = \frac{\sum_{i=1}^{n}(p_i - a_i)^2}{\sum_{i=1}^{n}(\bar{a} - a_i)^2}$$

R-square

A common way to summarize how well a linear regression model fits the data is via the coefficient of determination, or R2. This can be calculated as the square of the correlation between the observed y values and the predicted $\hat{y}$ values. Alternatively, it can also be calculated as follows where the summations are overall observations:

$$R^2 = \frac{\sum(\hat{y}_i - \bar{y})^2}{\sum(y_i - \bar{y})^2}$$

Thus, the proportion of variation in the forecast variable is accounted for (or explained) by the regression model.

If the predictions are close to the actual values, we would expect R2 to be close to one. On the other hand, if the predictions are unrelated to the actual values, then $R2=0$. In all cases, R2 lies between zero and one.

Adjusted R-square

R-square measures value depends upon the number of features in the dataset. When extra explanatory variables are added to the model the R-square automatically and spuriously increases. To address this issue adjusted R-square is used that adjusts for the number of explanatory terms in a model relative to the number of data points. On inclusion of a new explanatory variable, the adjusted R-square value will only increase if the improvement seen is not by chance. The value of adjusted R-square can be negative and is always less than or equal to R-square:

$$\bar{R}^2 = 1 - \left(1 - R^2\right)\frac{n-1}{n-p-1} = R^2 - \left(1 - R^2\right)\frac{p}{n-p-1}$$

Recommendation system

Evaluation of recommenders follows the same paradigm as for the supervised learning evaluation; keep aside a test dataset from the training data and evaluate the recommender based on the test data.

Score difference

We keep aside a test sample, where items already rated are kept aside as a test set. The training sample doesn't include the test ratings and the recommender estimates the ratings for those example ratings. The evaluation is based upon the difference between the actual ratings and predicted ratings. The difference can be defined in various ways, depending upon the requirement. Average difference or root mean square difference (to match below) are the most commonly used methods. Average difference is straightforward and intuitive, whereas root mean square differences can be used if we need to penalize larger difference in rating.

An illustration of the score difference is as follows:

Ratings	Item 1	Item 2	Item 3
Actual	4	5	3
Predicted	3	4	5
Difference	1	1	2

Average difference = (1 + 1+ 2)/3 = 1.33

Root mean square difference = sqrt((1*1 + 1*1 + 2*2)/3) = 1.414

As you can see the rms difference is higher as one difference is greater.

For a recommender that only provides binary outcomes, approach based on score difference cannot be used for providing future prediction, we need a different approach which is discussed next.

Precision and recall

In scenarios where preference rating is not required and just a list of recommendations is generated, we could use the previously discussed metric's precisions and recall can be used to measure the performance of a recommender. Let's assume that the recommender system provides a list of recommendations.

Precision is the proportion of top recommendations given that are good, and recall is the proportion of good recommendations that appear in the top recommendations.

We have to define *good* before we can calculate the metrics. Good can be a user-defined threshold value or it can be a default value. The default is an average preference value per user plus one standard deviation.

Clustering

The objective of clustering is to group similar things together. Similar items are grouped together into clusters, intra-cluster distances are minimized and inter-cluster distances are maximized.

The internal evaluation

When information obtained from the data that was used for clustering is used for evaluating the cluster health it is called internal evaluation. This method assigns higher scores for clusters with larger inter cluster distance and smaller intra cluster distance.

The intra-cluster distance

The intra-cluster distance is the sum of the square distance from the items of each cluster to its centroid.

The inter-cluster distance

The inter-cluster distance is the sum of the square distance between each cluster centroid.

The Davies–Bouldin index

The Davies-Bouldin index is an evaluation metric to measure cluster health and can be calculated using the following formula:

$$DB = \frac{1}{n} \sum_{i=1}^{n} \max_{i \neq j} \left(\frac{\sigma_i + \sigma_j}{d(c_i, c_j)} \right)$$

The clusters with smaller intra cluster distances and larger inter cluster distances will have a smaller Davies-Bouldin index and hence the candidate clusters with smallest index is considered the best cluster.

Here, n is the number of clusters, c_x is the centroid of cluster x, \sigma_x is the average distance of all elements in cluster x to centroid c_x, and d(c_i,c_j) is the distance between centroids c_i and c_j.

The Dunn index

The Dunn index aims to identify dense and well-separated clusters and is used to measure cluster health. The Dunn index is calculated by the following formula:

$$D = \min_{1 \leq i \leq n} \left\{ \min_{1 \leq j \leq n, i \neq j} \left\{ \frac{d(i, j)}{\max_{1 \leq k \leq n} d'(k)} \right\} \right\}$$

Here, *d(i,j)* represents the distance between clusters i and j, and d"{' }(k) measures the intra-cluster distance of cluster k. The inter-cluster distance d(i,j) between two clusters may be any number of distance measures, such as the distance between the centroids of the clusters. It is the ratio between the minimum inter-cluster distance to maximum intra-cluster distance and hence a larger Dunn Index represents higher cluster health.

The external evaluation

External evaluation is a form of measuring cluster health in which the results are evaluated based on data that was not used for clustering. This data can be known class labels or other external benchmarks. The benchmarks can consist of a set of preclassified items and these sets are often created by human experts. These evaluation methods measure how close the clustering is to the predetermined benchmark classes. However, it has recently been discussed among experts whether this is adequate for real data, or only on synthetic datasets with a factual ground truth. Since such classes can contain internal structures, the attributes present may not allow separation of clusters, or the classes themselves might contain anomalies. Additionally, from a knowledge discovery point of view, the reproduction of known knowledge may not necessarily be the intended result.

Some of the quality measures of a cluster algorithm using an external criterion are mentioned here.

The Rand index

The Rand index measures how similar the candidate clusters are to the predefined benchmark and the benchmark in this case is class labels. It can be viewed as a measure of the percentage of correct decisions made by grouping the instances together. It can be computed using the following formula:

$$RI = \frac{TP + TN}{TP + FP + FN + TN}$$

Here, TP is the number of true positives, TN is the number of true negatives, FP is the number of false positives, and FN is the number of false negatives. The Rand index weights the false positives and false negatives equally but that might not be suitable when a particular class is of more importance than the others. We can use the F-measure in such scenarios and it is discussed next.

F-measure

The F-measure can be used as an external evaluation measure in scenarios where false positive and false negatives need to be weighted differently. Precision and Recall be defined as follows:

$$P = \frac{TP}{TP + FP}$$

$$R = \frac{TP}{TP + FN}$$

F-measure can be computed using the following formula:

$$F_{\beta} = \frac{\left(\beta^2 + 1\right) \cdot P \cdot R}{\beta^2 \cdot P + R}$$

Summary

Machine learning adoption has increased in leaps and bounds in the last few years. Availability of data in the digital age, scalable platforms to process large amount of data, focus on intelligent applications, and the realization of the business values of machine learning has driven the growth. Machine learning is a vast field that requires continuing education to gain expertise. This chapter has introduced a few important concepts in machine learning but the knowledge gained is just the tip of the iceberg. I would encourage the reader to keep exploring and augmenting their knowledge. In the next chapter, we will discuss one of the first and most important parts of a machine learning project, feature engineering. Feature engineering deals with transforming and presenting data to the learning algorithm. We will cover some common techniques for feature extraction and dimensionality reduction.

3
Feature Engineering

This chapter discusses arguably the most important step in solving a machine learning problem. Feature engineering involves the preparation and representation of data on which the models can be trained. A good feature set is compulsory for the success of a modeling project. In this chapter, we are going to cover the following topics:

- Feature construction
- Feature extraction
- Feature selection
- Dimensionality reduction

Feature engineering

Let's start by understanding what is meant by feature engineering. Feature engineering is performed after data cleansing and preparation, before or even during model training. It aims to provide better representation of the data to the machine learning algorithm. Feature engineering as a process has multiple outcomes and can impact the overall modeling exercise in many ways. Feature engineering can be focused to increase model accuracy and generalization, decrease the computation requirements for large and wide datasets, and make the model simpler. Generally, a practitioner aims to do all of these. Feature engineering can be divided into four major tasks: feature construction, feature extraction, feature selection, and dimensionality reduction. We will discuss the four tasks shortly.

Before we discuss feature engineering, let's revisit the definition of features first:

- Raw data comes with many attributes. For example, for structured data such as a database table, the attributes would be the columns and for unstructured data, such as text, the attributes could be the words in the text.

- A feature is an attribute that is useful or meaningful to your machine learning problem. Some columns in a table could be meaningful and others, not. Similarly, for text classifications, stop words such as and, the, and so on are not useful and hence not used as features.

Now, let's briefly go through all the four tasks, and then we will discuss them in detail, giving examples.

- **Manual feature construction**: This is the process of constructing new features from raw data and existing features. For example, creating features such as sum, averages, and change percentages are constructed features. Quite a few times multiple features are combined to come up with constructed features. For example, we have two features, total number of transactions and successful transactions. An interesting feature that can be constructed is percentage of successful transactions. This new feature is an example of feature construction.

- **Automated feature extraction**: This is the process of building a set of new features from existing featuring. Some functional mappings between the old and new features are defined in order to create the new features out of existing features. Projecting data into a different dimension, as used by SVM kernels, is an example of feature extraction. Please note that sometimes the terminology is flexible and practitioners frequently use the same term *feature extraction* for both automated feature extraction and manual feature construction.

- **Feature selection**: This is the process of selecting a subset of relevant features from the existing features. There are two major strategies for feature selection, filter based and wrapper based. We will discuss these strategies later in the chapter.

- **Dimensionality reduction**: This is the process of reducing the number of features to be considered in the modeling process. The reasons for this are to improve computation performance and to address the curse of dimensionality. We can achieve dimensionality reduction by means of either feature selection or feature extraction.

Many of the techniques discussed in this chapter do not have direct support in Mahout and hence we will be discussing those using Python. In a real life scenario, one could sample a subset of the data and then use Python or any other tool of choice to experiment with the feature engineering and build a POC model and then build a full-fledged project in Mahout.

Feature construction

We refer to feature construction as a process in which the dataset is manually enhanced by either creating new features from existing ones or transforming the existing features. The constructed features may reflect the domain knowledge a practitioner has about the problem at hand, a rule of thumb that the practitioner tries regularly, or some common standard transformations of data. Manually constructed features created after understanding the data and the problem domain can lead to a good representation of the data and result in a simpler model with improved accuracy. Feature construction could lead to an increase in dimensionality of the features as we add new features.

Some examples of manual feature constructions are discussed here. We will use a common dataset for each of the examples, the Abalone dataset. The dataset has been downloaded from `https://archive.ics.uci.edu/ml/datasets/Abalone`, Sam Waugh (1995) *Extending and benchmarking Cascade-Correlation*, PhD thesis, Computer Science Department, University of Tasmania. You can download the data from the site or use the data in the source code folder supplied with this book. Headers have been added to the file to make it easier to understand.

Here is a description of the Abalone dataset:

Name	Data Type	Measurement	Description
Sex	nominal		M,F,I (infant)
Length	continuous	mm	Longest shell measurement
Diameter	continuous	mm	Perpendicular to length
Height	continuous	mm	Height with meat in shell
WholeWeight	continuous	grams	Whole abalone weight
ShuckedWeight	continuous	grams	Weight of only meat
VisceraWeight	continuous	grams	Gut weight (after bleeding)
ShellWeight	continuous	grams	Weight after being dried
Rings	integer		Adding 1.5 to the value gives the age in years

An abalone is a species of snail and in the dataset we have some measurements about each snail. Let's assume the objective of the study is to predict the sex, given the measurements. We will discuss how we can apply feature engineering, keeping the previously stated objective in mind.

The other dataset that we are going to consider is the adult dataset, mainly because it has a lot of categorical variables, so we can use it to discuss the feature construction techniques of categorical variables. You can either download the data from `https://archive.ics.uci.edu/ml/datasets/Adult` or use the file `adult.data.csv` present in the directory `learningApacheMahout/data/chapter3` that comes with this book's source code folder. A header line has been added to the data file that comes with this book repository.

The `adult.data.csv` file has already been preprocessed, but if you wish to use the original file `adult.data.txt` from the UCI repository then please follow the steps to prepare the instruction. Even if you wish to use the `adult.data.csv` file, it's a good idea to read through the process of cleaning the file. Let's look firstly at the raw file. Execute the `head` command displaying the first 5 lines of data.

```
head -5 adult.data.txt
```

The output is copied as follows. Note that the data has no header line and has white spaces between words that need to be removed:

```
39, State-gov, 77516, Bachelors, 13, Never-married, Adm-clerical, Not-in-
family, White, Male, 2174, 0, 40, United-States, <=50K
50, Self-emp-not-inc, 83311, Bachelors, 13, Married-civ-spouse, Exec-
managerial, Husband, White, Male, 0, 0, 13, United-States, <=50K
38, Private, 215646, HS-grad, 9, Divorced, Handlers-cleaners, Not-in-
family, White, Male, 0, 0, 40, United-States, <=50K
53, Private, 234721, 11th, 7, Married-civ-spouse, Handlers-cleaners,
Husband, Black, Male, 0, 0, 40, United-States, <=50K
28, Private, 338409, Bachelors, 13, Married-civ-spouse, Prof-specialty,
Wife, Black, Female, 0, 0, 40, Cuba, <=50K
```

To remove the white spaces, we will use **Sed**. Sed is a command line editor in Linux. Sed can perform pattern matching and search and replace operations. By default, Sed doesn't modify the original file, the output is directed to the standard output of Linux. We pass the search pattern `\s` that represents white spaces, the replace pattern is blank and the search and replace is done globally. The output of the `sed` command is saved to the new file `adult.data.csv`:

```
sed 's/\s//g' adult.data.txt > adult.data.csv
```

The next step is to encode the target variable. We will replace the value >50K with the value `True` and <=50K with `False`. To do this, we will again use the `sed` command, this time with the `-i` flag, which directs `sed` to make the changes directly in the input file:

```
sed -i 's/>50K/True/g' adult.data.csv
sed -i 's/<=50K/False/g' adult.data.csv
```

Let's view the file again, to see if the changes are being made as per our expectation. We run the `head` command, again this time on the file `adult.data.csv`:

```
head -5 adult.data.csv
```

As we can see in the output copied here, the white spaces have been removed and the target variable, which is the last column, is properly encoded:

```
39,State-gov,77516,Bachelors,13,Never-married,Adm-clerical,Not-in-
family,White,Male,2174,0,40,United-States,False
50,Self-emp-not-inc,83311,Bachelors,13,Married-civ-spouse,Exec-managerial
,Husband,White,Male,0,0,13,United-States,False
38,Private,215646,HS-grad,9,Divorced,Handlers-cleaners,Not-in-
family,White,Male,0,0,40,United-States,False
53,Private,234721,11th,7,Married-civ-spouse,Handlers-cleaners,Husband,Bla
ck,Male,0,0,40,United-States,False
28,Private,338409,Bachelors,13,Married-civ-spouse,Prof-specialty,Wife,Bla
ck,Female,0,0,40,Cuba,False
```

The last step is to add the header file. The preceding 1 in the match pattern instructs Sed to match only the first line. The caret sign ^ represent the start of line. So the command replaces the start of first line with the replacement text:

```
sed -i '1s/^/age,workclass,fnlwgt,education,education-num,marital-sta
tus,occupation,relationship,race,sex,capital-gain,capital-loss,hours-
perweek,native-country,IncomeGreaterThan50K\n/' adult.data.csv
```

We repeat a similar process for the Abalone dataset. For this file, we need to remove white spaces, if present, and add the header line. The downloaded file name is `abalone.data.txt` and the following commands will prepare the file for processing:

```
sed 's/\s//g' abalone.data.txt > abalone.data.csv
sed -i '1s/^/Sex,Length,Diameter,Height,WholeWeight,ShuckedWeight,Viscera
Weight,ShellWeight,Rings\n/' abalone.data.csv
```

The files are now ready for further processing; we can copy the file back to the data directory `learningApacheMahout/data/chapter3` of the code repository.

Here is a description of the adult dataset:

Name	Data Type	Description
Age	continuous	Age of the adult
workclass	categorical	Working class of the adult
fnlwgt	continuous	Final derived weight of the adult
education	categorical	Education level of the adult
education-num	continuous	Education level of the adult encoded as integer
marital-status	categorical	Marital Status of the adult
occupation	categorical	Occupation of the adult
relationship	categorical	Relationship of the adult
Race	categorical	Race of the adult
Sex	categorical	Gender of the adult
capital-gain	continuous	Capital gained by the adult
capital-loss	continuous	Capital lost by the adult
hours-per-week	continuous	Hours worked per week
native-country	categorical	Native country of the adult
IncomeGreaterThan50K	categorical	This column contains the value True or False according to whether the income of adult is greater than or less than 50 thousand per year.

The dataset has information about adults and the target variable is a categorical feature `IncomeGreaterThan50K`, which informs whether an adult has income above 50,000 or not.

Categorical features

As we have already discussed in *Chapter 2, Core Concepts in Machine Learning,* features that can only take few predefined and mostly fixed values are called categorical features. Let's discuss some feature construction techniques for categorical features.

Merging categories

Features such as zip code and industry can have a large number of distinct values. For a country like India, the number of distinct zip codes is around 150,000. There are a few problems with having a feature with this many values. First of all, any machine learning algorithm is going to struggle to derive insight from so many values. The training example for each distinct value might also be very few. To make the feature usable, we will have to reduce the number of categories, either by merging the different categories together or by creating different models for different subsets of categories. The second problem is that so many categorical values add unnecessary detail to the dataset. For example, to analyze the churn for a telecom subscriber, having data for an individual zip code is not helpful, when instead we could use the zip code data for the state level.

In the adults, data file, the feature education has 16 categories, which are as follows:

```
10th 11th 12th 1st-4th 5th-6th 7th-8th 9th Preschool Assoc-acdm Assoc-voc
Some-college HS-grad Bachelors Masters Prof-school Doctorate
```

Although 16 categories is not a large number of categories, and hence not very problematic, closer inspection reveals some natural grouping within these categories. The following categories: 10th, 11th, 12th, 1st-4th, 5th-6th, 7th-8th, 9th, Preschool can be naturally grouped together as lower education and categories Prof-school and Doctorate can be grouped as higher education. Let's investigate this variable in detail. Open the file CategoricalFeatureMerge.py in the directory learningApacheMahout/src/python/chapter3/src in your favorite text editor. To run the script, execute the following command from the same directory:

```
python CategoricalFeatureMerge.py
```

The code file imports pandas with the alias pd. pandas is an open source Python library providing high performance, easy-to-use data structures for data processing and analysis. It provides in-built functions for common data processing tasks, a few of which we will use in this chapter. To install pandas, execute the following command on the command line:

```
sudo pip install numpy pandas
```

Now, let's look at the code file. The script starts by importing the required packages and defining the class:

```
import pandas as pd
class CategoricalFeatureMerge:
def __init__(self):
pass
```

The next step is to read the csv into a data frame, for which we use pandas's `read_csv` function; `pandas, which` is referred to by the alias `pd`. A data frame is like a matrix that can contain columns of different data types:

```
df = pd.read_csv("../../../../data/chapter3/adult.data.csv")
```

We then use the `crosstab` function in panda to tabulate the education against the target variable `IncomeGreaterThan50K`:

```
print pd.crosstab(df['IncomeGreaterThan50K'],df['education'])
```

The output calculates the count of `False` and `True` in the `IncomeGreaterThan50K` variable for each category in education.

Here is a comparison of the education level with the target variable:

```
education against income
education             10th  11th  12th  1st-4th  5th-6th  7th-8th  9th  \
IncomeGreaterThan50K
False                  871  1115   400      162      317      606  487
True                    62    60    33        6       16       40   27

education             Assoc-acdm  Assoc-voc  Bachelors  Doctorate  HS-grad  \
IncomeGreaterThan50K
False                        802       1021       3134        107     8826
True                         265        361       2221        306     1675

education             Masters  Preschool  Prof-school  Some-college
IncomeGreaterThan50K
False                     764         51          153          5904
True                      959          0          423          1387
education                10th       11th         12th      1st-4th     5th-6th  \
```

We will convert the counts to percentages to make it easier to interpret. The apply function applies the defined operation to all the columns:

```
print pd.crosstab(df['IncomeGreaterThan50K'],df['education']).
apply(lambda r: r/r.sum(), axis=0)
```

The output is shown in the following figure:

```
education            10th      11th      12th    1st-4th   5th-6th  \
IncomeGreaterThan50K
False            0.933548  0.948936  0.923788  0.964286  0.951952
True             0.066452  0.051064  0.076212  0.035714  0.048048

education          7th-8th       9th  Assoc-acdm  Assoc-voc  Bachelors  \
IncomeGreaterThan50K
False             0.93808  0.947471    0.75164   0.738784   0.585247
True              0.06192  0.052529    0.24836   0.261216   0.414753

education        Doctorate   HS-grad   Masters  Preschool  Prof-school  \
IncomeGreaterThan50K
False              0.25908  0.840491  0.443413          1     0.265625
True               0.74092  0.159509  0.556587          0     0.734375

education       Some-college
IncomeGreaterThan50K
False               0.809765
True                0.190235
```

Comparison of education level with the target variable

The categories `Bachelors Masters` can be marked as `Medium` as around 50 percent of adults earn less than 50K. The categories `Prof-school` and `Doctorate` can be marked as `High`, as less than 70 percent adults earn more than 50K. With this, we have merged the categories into four different broad buckets with the potential of improving the model interpretability and performance. The following lines of code perform the merging of the categories for creating four different lists with their respective categories:

```
list_very_low_income_edu = ["10th","11th","12th","1st-4th","5th-
6th","7th-8th","9th","Preschool"]
list_low_income_edu = ["Assoc-acdm", "Assoc-voc", "Some-college", "HS-
grad"]
list_medium_income_edu = ["Bachelors", "Masters"]
list_high_income_edu = ["Prof-school", "Doctorate"]
```

If the current category is in the list, substitute it with the corresponding broader category:

```
df['education'].loc[df['education'].isin(list_very_low_income_edu)] =
'VeryLow'
df['education'].loc[df['education'].isin(list_low_income_edu)] = 'Low'
df['education'].loc[df['education'].isin(list_medium_income_edu)] =
'Medium'
df['education'].loc[df['education'].isin(list_high_income_edu)] = 'High'
```

Check whether the categories have been substituted:

```
print df['education'].unique()
```

The output is as follows:

```
['Medium' 'Low' 'VeryLow' 'High']
```

The last step is to save the modified file with the merged education categories to another csv file. The file `adult.data.merged.csv` is used for subsequent examples:

```
df.to_csv("../../../../data/chapter3/adult.data.merged.csv", index=False)
```

The preceding code and the codes discussed further in the chapter are very simplistic. The goal is to explain the concepts with easy-to-follow examples and hence simplicity is preferred.

Converting to binary variables

We can convert the categories in to a categorical variable to multiple binary variables. If a categorical feature has five categories, then we can create five features with zero representing the absence of that particular value and one representing the presence of that particular value. Conversion of categorical variables to binary variables is required if the particular learning algorithm doesn't support more than two categories.

We will use Python to convert the feature gender in `adult.data.csv` to binary features; any tool of choice can be used, but because Python is easy to use and explain, and this is an important skill for a data analyst to have, so we will use Python. Open the file `CategoricalFeatureToBinary.py` in the `learningApacheMahout/src/python/chapter3/src` directory in your favorite text editor. To execute the script, run the following command from the same directory.

```
python CategoricalFeatureToBinary.py
```

The first couple of lines import the required packages. To install `patsy`, please run the following command on the command line:

```
sudo pip install six patsy
```

The `patsy` library is a Python library that describes statistical models, and has some good functions for common data processing tasks:

```
import pandas as pd
import patsy
```

We then define the class `CategoricalFeatureToBinary`:

```
class CategoricalFeatureToBinary:
def __init__(self):
pass
```

We read the `adult.data.set.csv` into the data frame `df`:

```
df = pd.read_csv("../../../../data/chapter3/adult.data.csv")
```

Next, we print the column headers of the csv read:

```
print df.columns.values
```

The output is the following list of columns:

```
['age' 'workclass' 'fnlwgt' 'education' 'education-num' 'marital-status'
'occupation' 'relationship' 'race' 'sex' 'capital-gain' 'capital-loss'
'hours-per-week' 'native-country' 'IncomeGreaterThan50K']
```

Next, we convert the selected feature `sex` to binary features, we use the `dmatrix` function of the `patsy` package for it. The function takes the column name and returns a data frame based on the third parameter. The second parameter is the data frame itself. To convert multiple columns, use the + operator. For example, to convert `sex` and `workclass`, we need to pass `sex + workclass -1` as the first argument:

```
df_converted = patsy.dmatrix('sex - 1', df, return_type='dataframe')
```

The original file has the first five values of the feature `sex`, as follows:

Sex
Male
Male
Male
Male
Female

We print the output of the converted data; the first five lines are printed by default by the `head` function. `0` denotes `False` and `1` as `True`:

```
print df_converted.head()
```

The output is printed as follows:

```
sex[ Female] sex[ Male]
          0           1
          0           1
          0           1
          0           1
          1           0
```

The next step is to drop the selected column `sex`, as it is not needed in the original data anymore. The `inplace` argument drops the column in to the original frame itself and we don't need to assign it back, because the `axis` argument 1 represents columns and 0 represents rows:

```
df.drop('sex', inplace=True, axis=1)
```

Next, we concatenate the two data frames together so that the new binary columns are added to the original frame:

```
df = pd.concat([df_converted, df], axis=1)
```

We print the column headers again to check whether the new columns have been added. The new columns have been added to the start of the frame.

```
print df.columns.values
```

The output is as follows:

```
['sex[ Female]' 'sex[ Male]' 'age' 'workclass' 'fnlwgt' 'education'
 'education-num' 'marital-status' 'occupation' 'relationship' 'race'
 'capital-gain' 'capital-loss' 'hours-per-week' 'native-country'
 'IncomeGreaterThan50K']
```

The final step is to write the converted csv data frame to csv:

```
df.to_csv("../../../../data/chapter3/adult.data.converted_to_binary.csv",
index=False)
```

The conversion of categorical variables to binary features loses information, categories are going to be mutually exclusive as the same adult cannot be both male and female, and hence we should use this technique cautiously.

Converting to continuous variables

Categorical variables can also be converted to continuous variables. This approach can be used in a few scenarios. The first scenario — when the categories of a categorical feature can change over time, we can represent the categories in terms of their percentages of occurrence. For example, let's assume that the income study in the future will include other `education` categories. Industries change over a period of time and so does the demand for education levels and specialization. It would not be incorrect to assume that high-paying education jobs would continue to get higher wages at any particular point of time. Hence, rather than using the actual categories in the feature set, we could calculate the percent of adults getting greater than 50K and use it as a feature. This will take care of new categories being introduced and also the variation in the demand for a specific education level over a period of time.

Open the file `CategoricalFeatureToPercentages.py` in the directory `learningApacheMahout/src/python/chapter3/src` in your favorite editor. To execute the script execute the following command from the same directory:

```
python CategoricalFeatureToPercentages.py
```

First, we import the required package:

```
import pandas as pd
```

We read the adult dataset with merged education categories. It will be easier to explain with a smaller number of categories:

```
df = pd.read_csv("../../../../data/chapter3/adult.data.merged.csv")")
print pd.crosstab(df['IncomeGreaterThan50K'],df['education']).
apply(lambda r: r/r.sum(), axis=0)print df['sex'].head()
```

The output is as printed here:

education	High	Low	Medium	VeryLow
IncomeGreaterThan50K				
False	0.262892	0.817796	0.550721	0.942629
True	0.737108	0.182204	0.449279	0.057371

We can now replace the category High with 0.737108, Medium with 0.449279, and so on.

Another technique is to add new features pivoting a continuous variable on the categories in a categorical feature. This is mostly done with time stamped data.

Continuous features

We will discuss a few common transformations for continuous features. Continuous features can take any value in their range.

Binning

We can bin continuous features using thresholds. Few learning algorithms such as naïve Bayes only work with categorical features and for these scenarios, discretization or binning is important. Binning of variables can be both supervised as well as unsupervised.

Unsupervised binning has two common methods, equal frequency and equal width binning. In equal frequency binning, each bin has equal number of instances, whereas in equal width binning, the bins are chosen to have the same interval. Another useful method of unsupervised binning is to use a clustering algorithm to identify the natural boundaries of the feature and use those boundaries as the bins. Clustering methods like k-means, agglomerative clustering, and so on can be used.

Supervised binning is performed using the information from the target variable. The thresholds are decided based on how well the splits divide the target variable. For example, we can use a decision tree and train the tree on each feature that we want to bin; the decision tree will provide the splitting points and we can use the same to define the thresholds. More generally, rather than using a tree, we can use some measures such as Information Gain or the Gini index to decide the split points.

We will discuss a small example of equal frequency binning. Open the file ContinuousFeatureBinning.py from the same location as all the examples above. This script uses scipy and scikit-learn, these are scientific computing packages in Python. To install the packages please execute the following command:

```
sudo pip install scipy scikit-learn
```

We read the adult data file into a data frame df and then call the function describe() on the age feature. The describe function returns the summary statistics of the feature:

```
df = pd.read_csv("../../../../data/chapter3/adult.data.csv")
print df['age'].describe()
```

The output is as follows:

```
count      32561.000000
mean          38.581647
std           13.640433
min           17.000000
25%           28.000000
```

50%	37.000000
75%	48.000000
max	90.000000

We have four equal frequency bins, [17, 28], (28, 37], (37, 48], and (48, 90], we will replace these with labels `Young`, `Adult`, `MiddleAge`, `Old`. We converted the continuous feature `Age` into a categorical feature:

```
df['age'] = pd.qcut(x=df['age'],q=4,labels=['Young','Adult','MiddleAge','Old'])
print df['age'].unique()
```

The output is `['Young' 'Adult' 'MiddleAge' 'Old']`.

Binarization

We can create binary feature out of continuous feature by using a threshold. A binary feature as the name suggests has two distinct values, most commonly (`0`, `1`) and (`True`, `False`). Values greater than a particular threshold can take one of the two values and values less than equal to the threshold can take the other. Let's see this technique in practice on the `age` variable in adult dataset. Open the file `ContinuousFeatureBinarization.py` from the same location as all the examples above.

We read the adult dataset into the data frame `df`:

```
df = pd.read_csv("../../../../data/chapter3/adult.data.csv")
```

We print the first five values of the feature `age`:

```
print df['age'].head()
```

The output of the command is as follows:

```
0    39
1    50
2    38
3    53
4    28
```

We call the Binarizer function passing the threshold 40, values above 40 will be marked `1`, and values below 40 marked `0`:

```
binarizer = preprocessing.Binarizer(threshold=40)
print binarizer.transform(df['age'])[0:5]
```

The output is `[0 1 0 1 0]`.

Feature standardization

In real life data, the features are more often than not on different scales. Many machine learning algorithms will not work properly with datasets of different scales. An important concept in feature construction is to standardize the range of a feature by scaling it. We can either rescale the features or standardize the feature according to the mean or scale to unit length. This process of feature standardization is also referred to as feature normalization.

Rescaling

One way to standardize data is to rescale it by subtracting each value by the min and dividing by the range of the feature. This ensures that the values are between [0, 1]:

$$x_{new} = \frac{x - x_{min}}{x_{max} - x_{min}}$$

Mean standardization

Standardization of data refers to the transformation that enables the feature to have a mean of zero and a variance of one. For each value in a feature, we subtract the value by the mean of the feature and divide by the standard deviation:

$$x_{new} = \frac{x - \mu}{\sigma}$$

Scaling to unit norm

Each value in a feature is divided by its norm. Depending on the use case, it could be L1 or L2 or any other norm. After division by the norm, the feature itself has a norm of one.

 A norm is a function that assigns a strictly positive length or size to each vector in a vector space, other than the zero vector that has a length zero assigned to it.

Open the file `ContinousFeatureStandardization.py`. This code file uses the package `numpy` and `scikit learn`. The `scikit learn` package is a machine learning package in Python and implements many machine learning algorithms as built-in modules. The `numpy` package is a powerful package for scientific computing in Python. To install both, execute the following command on the command line:

```
sudo pip install numpy scikit-learn
```

First, we will discuss the code for rescaling. The object `min_max_scaler` will transform the feature `age` to a range of [0, 1]:

```
df = pd.read_csv("../../../../data/chapter3/adult.data.csv")
min_max_scaler = preprocessing.MinMaxScaler()
X_train_minmax = min_max_scaler.fit_transform(df['age'].astype(float))
print min(X_train_minmax),max(X_train_minmax)
```

The minimum is 0 and the maximum is 1.

Next, we discuss the code for mean standardization. The function scale subtracts the mean from each value and divides by standard deviation:

```
df = pd.read_csv("../../../../data/chapter3/abalone.data.csv")
test= (preprocessing.scale(df['Height']))
print test.mean()
print test.std()
```

The mean of the transformed variable is ~0 and variance is 1.

Next, we will discuss the code to transform the feature to unit norm. The transformed feature will have a norm of 1:

```
weights = sorted(np.arange(float(14), 0.05, -1.0))
weight_norm = np.linalg.norm(weights)
weights = weights/weight_norm
print np.linalg.norm(weights)
```

Feature transformation derived from the problem domain

The most powerful feature transformations are the ones guided by domain knowledge of the problem at hand and understanding of data gained from data exploration. The list of such transformations is huge and even the largest list can't be exhaustive. I am discussing some of the common problem-driven transformations.

Ratios

Quite often, a change in a variable over a period of time can be a very predicting feature. For example, in churn modeling, the decline of a usage metric like logins over a period of time is a very important predictor. Another example of ratios would be between features and the ratio of failed transaction by total number of transactions.

Frequency

Frequency of events over a period of time is always an interesting transformation for event-based time-stamped data.

Aggregate transformations

Aggregate transformations such as sum, average, minimum, and maximum over a group are the staples of most feature sets.

Normalization

So far, we have seen normalization of a column or feature. Another option to explore is row normalization by a metric.

Mathematical transformations

Another important feature construction technique is to apply appropriate mathematical transformations on the features. The motivation behind this is to decrease the skew and variance of the feature. Common mathematical transformations are log transformations with different bases, exponential transformations, and so on.

Feature extraction

Feature extraction is the process of automatic construction of new set of features from an existing one. For example, take a feature set and project it into a higher dimensional coordinates, the motivation being that the data might have a plane of separation in a higher dimension. Let's see an example using two dimensional data, in the plot to the left, the two classes represented by * and o cannot be separated by a straight line. If the data is projected to a three-dimensional plane, we can see that the two classes can be separated by a plane:

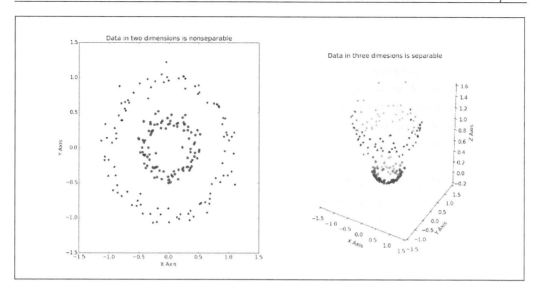

The line of separation in two dimensions is represented by a plane in three dimensions and as a hyper plane in more than three dimensions. The plot on the left of the image shows a plane separating the data, and the plot on the right projects the separation into two dimensions:

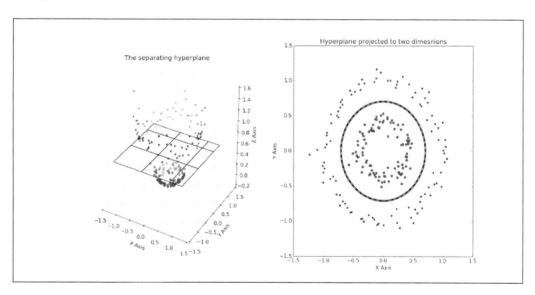

By projecting data from a lower dimension into a higher dimension, we can solve problems that cannot be solved by linearity in the lower dimension. One drawback of the approach is that projection of data from lower dimension to a higher one is computationally intensive and cannot scale one larger data. A kernel trick is one of the ways of solving the problem. A kernel is a function that computes the dot products into a higher dimension, while remaining in the lower dimension. By using a kernel, we can implicitly transform a dataset into a higher dimensional space without explicitly calculating the projection.

Feature extraction is an automated process. There are a number of generic feature construction methods that can be performed, based on the objective and data. Some common feature extraction techniques are as follows:

- Clustering-based feature extraction
- Linear transforms of the input variables such as PCA/SVD and so on
- Spectral transforms like Fourier transforms
- Applying simple functions to subsets of variables, such as algebraic computation on more than one feature

Feature selection

The primary goal of feature selection is to select a subset of features from the total feature set that can be used to build a good predictor with increased performance and generalization. It is not aimed at finding all the relevant features or reducing the dimensionality of the feature set, though both could be outcomes of the process. The difference between dimensionality reduction and feature selection is that the purpose of feature selection is to select the predictor with greater predictive power, whereas dimensionality reduction is aimed at a concise representation of the data. The similarity between them is that both lead to reduced number of features.

Feature selection can be both supervised and unsupervised. Feature selection could be filtered-based or wrapper-based.

Filter-based feature selection

Features are ranked according to an importance measure such as Information Gain and Chi-Squared test, and a subset of features can be selected, based on a threshold. The threshold-based rejection of features is aimed at selecting only those features that have a strong correlation with the target variable.

There are a few disadvantages of filter-based feature selection. The first problem is caused by correlated features. If a set of correlated features also have a strong correlation with the target variable, all of them will be selected as strong features but the correlated features will not add any extra information. The correlated features will repeat the same information. For example, we might have a telecom provider with one calling plan for the entire subscriber base. In this scenario, predictors *total minutes called* and *total amount charged* are going to be highly correlated and only one should be in the feature set. Both features have a strong correlation with the target variable churn. A filter-based feature selection mechanism will select both the features. Before implementing a filter-based feature selection, it is important to handle the correlated features.

Another problem with filter-based feature selection is that it cannot take into account interaction between multiple features to compute feature importance. Two features could independently have a very weak correlation with the target variable but when combined, they might be able to explain the target variable very well. Filter-based feature selection cannot capture this interaction and hence both these features will be ignored.

Wrapper-based feature selection

This method assesses subsets of features, according to their usefulness to a given predictor. This method uses the machine learning algorithm that we are modeling with to score subsets of features, according to their predictive power. Wrapper-based feature selection has the advantage of taking into account the interaction between features that filter-based methods cannot. The disadvantage of wrapper-based feature selection is that it can be computationally expensive. But there are different search techniques that can mitigate this drawback. Many search techniques can be used to do this, such as recursive feature elimination or backward selection, forward selection, step-wise selection, and so on. Each search technique might converge to an optimum set of features. We briefly introduce the main concepts in the wrapper-based feature selection; note that the actual implementations have slight variations over the main concepts.

Backward selection

In backward selection initially all the features in the feature set is used to fit the model. After the model is fir the each features is ranked according to its importance to the model. During each iteration of the algorithm, the top N raked features are retained, the model is refitted and its performance is assessed. The value of N with the best performance of the model is determined and the top N predictors are then used to fit the final model. Thus at the end of the process we are left with top N features for building the model.

Forward selection

In the forward selection algorithm, we start with the null set and sequentially add features from the feature set. The feature score is recomputed and finally, the subset with the best performance is retained.

Recursive feature elimination

Recursive feature elimination works by by recursively considering smaller and smaller sets of features. Initially the model is trained on all the features and weights are assigned to each one of them, the weights are assigned by some estimations, like the coefficients of a linear model, weights according to Information gain etc. The features with the smallest weights are pruned from the set features and the model trained again. This procedure is recursively repeated on the pruned set until the desired number of features are eventually reached.

Embedded feature selection

This search scheme is similar to the wrapper-based scheme, the difference being that the embedded method incorporates variable selection as part of model training. For example, random forest, gradient boosted trees, and so on, embedded feature selection is tied to a machine learning algorithm.

Generally, using the models with the embedded feature selection is more efficient compared to algorithms where the feature section is done externally using some search routines. With embedded feature selection typically we get the advantage of selecting good features with parameter optimization and model selection. The model is optimized and features selected using the same objective function.

Dimensionality reduction

Dimensionality reduction deals with representing the features into a more concise form. Dimensionality reduction can be achieved either through feature selection or feature extraction. The motivation can be both computation efficiency and to mitigate the curse of dimensionality. In simple terms, as the dimension or the number of features increases, the amount of data required to model the problem at hand increases exponentially. Collecting and processing large amount of data might not be possible and hence it is important to reduce the number of features or dimensionality of the dataset. One of the most common ways of reducing the dimensionality of the feature set is to use PCA.

Intuitively, PCA tries to find the simplest representation of a dataset. It projects data into a different coordinate system to provide a concise representation of data. The output of PCA is data that is represented as principal components. The term principal component denotes new variables (or coordinate systems) that we choose to describe our data in a more concise or convenient way. All principal components must satisfy two conditions:

- They must be perpendicular to each other. This means principal components are not linearly correlated between each other. This is one major advantage of using PCA; it removes correlated variables. The presence of correlated variables degrades the performance of algorithms such as logistic regression.

- The principal components must be pointed in the direction of the largest variance of data. Thus data must have the largest variance along the axes of component 1, and the 2nd largest variance along the axes of component 2, and so on. So the first component will be the most significant, the second, the second most significant, and so on. We can use this information to reduce the dimensionality. If, say, 99 percent of the variance such as explained by n principal components of a dataset that has k dimensions, where k is greater than n, then we can use the n principal components in reducing the dimensionality by k-n.

Now, let's see an example; open the file PCAExample.py in an editor like vi or gedit. The code file can be found under the same directory as the other code files learningApacheMahout/src/python/chapter3/src.

In this example, we are going to work with the Iris dataset. This dataset comes prepackaged with the scikit learn package we installed in the previous example. The dataset has four features: sepal length, sepal width, petal length, and petal width, and the class label that represents the species of the flower. The first step is to load the data:

```
df = datasets.load_iris()
```

The object df has two attributes df.data. And df.target; df.data holds the training data and df.target the class labels.

Let's see the sample data in df.data, as discussed earlier, it has four features. A few lines are copied, as follows:

```
[ 5.1   3.5   1.4   0.2]
[ 4.9   3.    1.4   0.2]
[ 4.7   3.2   1.3   0.2]
[ 4.6   3.1   1.5   0.2]
```

We have three target variables, denoted by 0, 1, and 2.

The next step is to create the `DecisionTreeClassifier` object. This object will be used to train a decision tree with the training data:

```
model = DecisionTreeClassifier()
```

Once we have created the object, the next step is to train the model. The `fit()` method takes the training data as the first argument and the target labels as the second argument:

```
model.fit(df.data, df.target)
```

The model has been created, now we need to check the efficacy of the model. We take the actual class labels in the variable expected and the class label predicted by the model in the variable predicted. The `predict()` function returns the predictions for the data passed as argument:

```
expected = df.target
predicted = model.predict(df.data)
```

The next step is to produce the efficacy metrics. The function `classification_report()` as well as `confusion_matrix()` takes as input the actual and the predicted value and print the performance metric:

```
print(metrics.classification_report(expected, predicted))
print(metrics.confusion_matrix(expected, predicted))
```

The output is copied here, we can see that using all the features we were able to get a prefect prediction:

```
precision  recall  f1-score   support

   0   1.00     1.00     1.00       50
   1   1.00     1.00     1.00       50
   2   1.00     1.00     1.00       50

[50  0  0]
[0  50  0]
[0  0  50]
```

Now, we will perform PCA on the original dataset and check the variance captured by each of the principal components. First, we create the PCA object and then get the components using the `fit_transform()` method:

```
principal_components = PCA()
pca_data = principal_components.fit_transform(df.data)
```

Let's check the explained variance of the principal components. The attribute `explained_variance_ratio_` holds the value:

```
print principal_components.explained_variance_ratio_
```

The output is copied here, we can see that the first component explains 92 percent of the variance:

```
[ 0.92461621  0.05301557  0.01718514  0.00518309]
```

We will repeat these steps to create a decision tree; this time, we will use the first principal component instead of the raw data. We have reduced the dimensionality of the problem from four to one, while retaining 92 percent of the original information. This is a good trade-off.

Since the rest of the steps are similar to what we discussed, I will only discuss the part where we are training the model. We select the first column `pca_data`:

```
model.fit(pca_data[:,[0]],df.target)
```

The efficacy of the new model is the same as the model built with the original data. This is a very simple example, but in real life scenarios with thousands of dimensions, PCA can make a big difference. We can reduce the dimensionality of the data, which in turn reduces the number of training examples required for building a good model and thus significantly reduces the amount of time and computation resources required for training.

Summary

In this chapter, we discussed the common techniques of feature engineering. The concepts and techniques discussed are very important; anyone working in data analysis will use these techniques regularly. A robust feature engineering process is imperative for a successful machine learning project. The better we represent data to an algorithm, the better its efficacy.

Chapter 1, *Introduction to Mahout*, *Chapter 2*, *Core Concepts in Machine Learning* and *Chapter 3*, *Feature Engineering* have provided a strong introduction to the basics of Mahout and machine learning. Now, we will start discussing the machine learning algorithms in detail. In the next chapter, we will discuss classification algorithms implemented in Mahout, covering both the concepts and practical examples.

4

Classification with Mahout

One of the most widely used tasks in machine learning is to predict discrete outcomes or classes of future data instances, using historical data. It is a very popular branch of supervised learning, and a wide variety of problems can be solved using this paradigm. Questions such as whether to approve a loan to someone or determining the probability of a telecom subscriber not renewing the contract can be answered using classification algorithms. In this chapter, we are going to discuss some of the important classification algorithms in Mahout. We will learn about the following classification algorithms:

- Logistic regression
- Random forest
- naïve Bayes

Classification

We discussed supervised learning in detail in *Chapter 2, Core Concepts in Machine Learning*. Here, we are going to put into action some of the practices we learned. The most critical parts of any machine learning task are data exploration, cleaning, and feature representation. The process involves exploring the data, addressing the anomalies in the data, extracting features, feature selection, and feature reduction, if required. Almost 70 percent of the time in any data analytics project is spent in feature engineering, and it is the most important part of the analytical process.

Then comes the task of training models; selection of which machine learning algorithms to use is mostly guided by the available data and the objective of the problem we are about to solve.

Machine learning algorithms can be separated into two groups, based on the capability of a user to see how a model arrives at its predicted output. If we can deduce from the model how a particular prediction was done by the algorithm, we can derive insights from it.

White box models

The process of prediction is very transparent and well-understood by the user. When we say the process of prediction, we don't mean the internal working of the algorithm but after the model is trained, what factors lead to a particular prediction. This helps us in deducing insights for a particular problem area. For example, a decision tree, which is a white box technique, can provide us with rules after training the model. For example, if we are building a decision tree, which predicts classes for outdoors and indoors based on weather and temperature, we could get the following rules:

```
if weather='sunny' and temperature='medium' then class 'outdoors'
if weather ='overcast' and temperature='low' then class 'indoors'
```

Black box models

The process of prediction is opaque to the user. Though the logic of the algorithm may be known, how it predicts a particular instance is hard to understand. Say if we used SVM, which is a black box algorithm that classifies data by drawing a hyperplane, for the aforementioned problem, we would get a prediction for each row or instance but no insights would be derived easily giving reasons for of the prediction.

Logistic regression

Logistic regression is a probabilistic classification model. It provides the probability of a particular instance belonging to a class. It is used to predict the probability of binary outcomes. Logistic regression is computationally inexpensive, is relatively easier to implement, and can be interpreted easily.

Logistic regression belongs to the class of **discriminative** models. The other class of algorithms is **generative** models. Let's try to understand the differences between the two. Suppose we have some input data represented by X and a target variable Y, the learning task obviously is $P(Y \mid X)$, finding the conditional probability of Y occurring given X. A generative model concerns itself with learning the joint probability of $P(Y, X)$, whereas a discriminative model will directly learn the conditional probability of $P(Y \mid X)$ from the training set. This is the actual objective of classification. A generative model first learns $P(Y, X)$, and then gets to $P(Y \mid X)$ by conditioning on X by using Bayes' theorem.

In more intuitive terms, generative models first learn the distribution of the data, then they model how the data is actually generated. However, discriminative models don't try to learn the underlying data distribution; they are concerned with finding the decision boundaries for the classification. Since generative models learn the distribution, it is possible to generate synthetic samples of X, Y. This is not possible with discriminative models.

Some common examples of generative and discriminative models are as follows:

- Generative: naïve Bayes, Latent Dirichlet allocation
- Discriminative: Logistic regression, SVM, Neural networks

Logistic regression belongs to the family of statistical techniques called regression. For regression problems and few other optimization problems, we first define a hypothesis, then define a cost function, and optimize it using an optimization algorithm such as Gradient descent. The optimization algorithm tries to find the regression coefficient, which best fits the data. Let's assume that the target variable is Y and the predictor variable or feature is X. Any regression problem starts with defining the hypothesis function, for example, an equation of the predictor variable $\alpha + \beta x$, defines a cost function and then tweaks the weights; in this case, α and β are tweaked to minimize or maximize the cost function by using an optimization algorithm.

For logistic regression, the predicted target needs to fall between zero and one. We start by defining the hypothesis function for it:

$$h_\theta(x) = f(\theta^T x)$$

$$f(z) = \frac{1}{(1+e^{-z})}$$

Here, *f(z)* is the sigmoid or logistic function that has a range of zero to one, **x** is a matrix of features, and θ is the vector of weights. The next step is to define the cost function, which measures the difference between predicted and actual values.

$$Cost(h_\theta(x), y) = \{-y \log(h_\theta(x)) - (1-y)\log(1 - h_\theta(x))\}$$

$$J(\theta) = -\frac{1}{m}\left(\sum_{i=1}^{m} Cost(h_\theta(x^i), y^i)\right)$$

$$= -\frac{1}{m}\left[\sum_{i=1}^{m} y^i \log h_\theta(x^i) + (1-y^i)\log(1 - \log h_\theta(x^i))\right]$$

The objective of the optimization algorithm here is to find $\min_\theta (J(\theta))$. This fits the regression coefficients so that the difference between predicted and actual target values are minimized. We will discuss gradient descent as the choice for the optimization algorithm shortly. To find the local minimum of a function using gradient descent, one takes steps proportional to the negative of the gradient of that function at the current point.

$$\text{Repeat} \left\{ \theta_j := \theta_j - \alpha \sum_{1=1}^{m} \left(h_\theta \left(x^i \right) - y^i \right) x_j^i \right\}$$

This will give us the optimum value of vector θ, once we achieve the stopping criteria. The stopping criteria is when the change in the weight vectors falls below a certain threshold, although sometimes it could be set to a predefined number of iterations.

Logistic regression falls into the category of white box techniques and can be interpreted. We will see how to interpret a logistic regression later on in the chapter.

Features or variables are of two major types, categorical and continuous, defined as follows:

- Categorical variable: This is a variable or feature that can take on a limited, and usually fixed, number of possible values. Example, variables such as industry, zip code, and country are categorical variables.

- Continuous variable: This is a variable that can take on any value between its minimum value and maximum value or range. Example, variable such as age, price, and so on, are continuous variables.

Mahout logistic regression command line

Mahout employs a modified version of gradient descent called stochastic gradient descent. The previous optimization algorithm that we discussed, gradient ascent, uses the whole dataset on each update of the weights. This is fine when the number of training instances are not huge, but with larger data volumes having a large number of training instances and features gradient ascent will have scalability issues. An alternative to gradient ascent is to update the weights using, only one instance at a time. This is the approach used in Mahout and is known as stochastic gradient ascent. It is an example of an online learning algorithm. We can incrementally update the classifier as new data comes in, rather than wait for the data and then update the weights in batch processing mode

We will now train and test a logistic regression algorithm using Mahout. We will also discuss both command line and code examples. The first step is to get the data and explore it.

Getting the data

The dataset required for this chapter is included in the code repository that comes with this book. It is present in the `learningApacheMahout/data/chapter4` directory. If you wish to download the data, the same can be downloaded from the UCI link. The UCI is a repository for many datasets for machine learning. You can check out the other datasets available for further practice via this link `http://archive.ics.uci.edu/ml/datasets.html`.

Create a folder in your home directory with the following command:

```
cd $HOME
mkdir bank_data
cd bank_data
```

Download the data in the `bank_data` directory:

```
wget http://archive.ics.uci.edu/ml/machine-learning-databases/00222/bank-additional.zip
```

Unzip the file using whichever utility you like, we use `unzip`:

```
unzip bank-additional.zip
cd bank-additional
```

We are interested in the file `bank-additional-full.csv`. Copy the file to the `learningApacheMahout/data/chapter4` directory. The file is semicolon delimited and the values are enclosed by ", it also has a header line with column name. We will use `sed` to preprocess the data. The `sed` editor is a very powerful editor in Linux and the command to use it is as follows:

```
sed -e 's/STRING_TO_REPLACE/STRING_TO_REPLACE_IT/g' fileName > Output_fileName
```

For inplace editing, the command is as follows:

```
sed -i 's/STRING_TO_REPLACE/STRING_TO_REPLACE_IT/g'
```

Command to replace ; with , and remove " are as follows:

```
sed -e 's/;/,/g' bank-additional-full.csv > input_bank_data.csv
sed -i 's/"//g' input_bank_data.csv
```

The dataset contains demographic and previous campaign-related data about a client and the outcome of whether or not the client did subscribed to the term deposit. We are interested in training a model, which can predict whether a client will subscribe to a term deposit, given the input data.

The following table shows various input variables along with their types:

Column name	Description	Variable type
Age	This represents the age of the Client	Numeric
Job	This represents their type of the job, for example, entrepreneur, housemaid, management	Categorical
Marital	This represents their marital status	Categorical
Education	This represents their education level	Categorical
Default	States whether the client has defaulted on credit	Categorical
Housing	States whether the client has a housing loan	Categorical
Loan	States whether the client has a personal loan	Categorical
contact	States the contact communication type	Categorical
Month	States the last contact month of the year	Categorical
day_of_week	States the last contact day of the week	Categorical
duration	States the last contact duration, in seconds	Numeric
campaign	This represents the number of contacts	Numeric
Pdays	This represents the number of days that passed since the last contact	Numeric
previous	This represents the number of contacts performed before this campaign	Numeric
poutcome	This represents the outcome of the previous marketing campaign	Categorical
emp.var.rate	States the employment variation rate - quarterly indicator	Numeric
cons.price.idx	States the consumer price index - monthly indicator	Numeric
cons.conf.idx	States the consumer confidence index - monthly indicator	Numeric
euribor3m	States the euribor three month rate - daily indicator	Numeric
nr.employed	This represents the number of employees - quarterly indicator	Numeric

Model building via command line

Mahout uses command line implementation of logistic regression. We will first build a model using the command line implementation. Logistic regression does not have a map to reduce implementation, but as it uses stochastic gradient descent, it is pretty fast, even for large datasets. The Mahout Java class is `OnlineLogisticRegression` in the `org.mahout.classifier.sgd` package.

Splitting the dataset

To split a dataset, we can use the Mahout split command. Let's look at the split command arguments as follows:

```
mahout split --help
```

--input (-i) input	Path to job input directory.
--trainingOutput (-tr) trainingOutput	The training data output directory
--testOutput (-te) testOutput	The test data output directory
--testSplitSize (-ss) testSplitSize	The number of documents held back as test data for each category
--testSplitPct (-sp) testSplitPct	The % of documents held back as test data for each category
--splitLocation (-sl) splitLocation	Location for start of test data expressed as a percentage of the input file size (0=start, 50=middle, 100=end
--randomSelectionSize (-rs) randomSelectionSize	The number of items to be randomly selected as test data
--randomSelectionPct (-rp) randomSelectionPct	Percentage of items to be randomly selected as test data when using mapreduce mode
--charset (-c) charset	The name of the character encoding of the input files (not needed if using SequenceFiles)
--sequenceFiles (-seq)	Set if the input files are sequence files. Default is false
--method (-xm) method	The execution method to use: sequential or mapreduce. Default is mapreduce

We need to remove the first line before running the split command, as the file contains the header file and the split command doesn't make any special allowances for header lines. It will land in any line in the split file.

We first remove the header line from the `input_bank_data.csv` file.

```
sed -i '1d' input_bank_data.csv
mkdir input_bank
cp input_bank_data.csv input_bank
```

Logistic regression in Mahout is implemented for single-machine execution. We set the variable `MAHOUT_LOCAL` to instruct Mahout to execute in the local mode.

```
export MAHOUT_LOCAL=TRUE

mahout split --input input_bank --trainingOutput train_data --testOutput
test_data -xm sequential --randomSelectionPct 30
```

This will create different datasets, with the split based on number passed to the argument `--randomSelectionPct`. The split command can run in both Hadoop and the local file system. For current execution, it runs in the local mode on the local file system and splits the data into two sets, 70 percent as train in the `train_data` directory and 30 percent as test in `test_data` directory.

Next, we restore the header line to the train and test files as follows:

```
sed -i '1s/^/age,job,marital,education,default,housing,loan,contact,month
,day_of_week,duration,campaign,pdays,previous,poutcome,emp.var.rate,cons.
price.idx,cons.conf.idx,euribor3m,nr.employed,y\n/' train_data/input_
bank_data.csv
```

```
sed -i '1s/^/age,job,marital,education,default,housing,loan,contact,month
,day_of_week,duration,campaign,pdays,previous,poutcome,emp.var.rate,cons.
price.idx,cons.conf.idx,euribor3m,nr.employed,y\n/' test_data/input_bank_
data.csv
```

Train the model command line option

Let's have a look at some important and commonly used parameters and their descriptions:

```
mahout trainlogistic --help

--help print this list
--quiet be extra quiet
--input "input directory from where to get the training data"
--output "output directory to store the model"
--target "the name of the target variable"
--categories "the number of target categories to be considered"
--predictors "a list of predictor variables"
--types "a list of predictor variables types (numeric, word or text)"
--passes "the number of times to pass over the input data"
--lambda "the amount of coefficient decay to use"
```

```
--rate  "learningRate the learning rate"
--noBias "do not include a bias term"
--features "the number of internal hashed features to use"

mahout trainlogistic --input train_data/input_bank_data.csv --output
model --target y --predictors age job marital education default housing
loan contact month day_of_week duration campaign pdays previous poutcome
emp.var.rate cons.price.idx cons.conf.idx euribor3m nr.employed --types
n w w w w w w w w w n n n n w n n n n n --features 20 --passes 100 --rate
50 --categories 2
```

We pass the input filename and the output folder name, identify the target variable name using --target option, the predictors using the --predictors option, and the variable or predictor type using --types option. Numeric predictors are represented using 'n', and categorical variables are predicted using 'w'. Learning rate passed using --rate is used by gradient descent to determine the step size for each descent. We pass the maximum number of passes over data as 100 and categories as 2.

The output is given below, which represents 'y', the target variable, as a sum of predictor variables multiplied by coefficient or weights. As we have not included the --noBias option, we see the intercept term in the equation:

```
y ~

-990.322*Intercept Term + -131.624*age + -11.436*campaign
+ -990.322*cons.conf.idx + -14.006*cons.price.idx +
-15.447*contact=cellular + -9.738*contact=telephone + 5.943*day_
of_week=fri + -988.624*day_of_week=mon + 10.551*day_of_week=thu +
11.177*day_of_week=tue + -131.624*day_of_week=wed + -8.061*default=no
+ 12.301*default=unknown + -131.541*default=yes + 6210.316*duration
+ -17.755*education=basic.4y + 4.618*education=basic.6y +
8.780*education=basic.9y + -11.501*education=high.school +
0.492*education=illiterate + 17.412*education=professional.course +
6202.572*education=university.degree + -979.771*education=unknown
+ -189.978*emp.var.rate + -6.319*euribor3m + -21.495*housing=no +
-14.435*housing=unknown + 6210.316*housing=yes + -190.295*job=admin.
+ 23.169*job=blue-collar + 6202.200*job=entrepreneur +
6202.200*job=housemaid + -3.208*job=management + -15.447*job=retired +
1.781*job=self-employed + 11.396*job=services + -6.637*job=student +
6202.572*job=technician + -9.976*job=unemployed + -4.575*job=unknown
+ -12.143*loan=no + -0.386*loan=unknown + -197.722*loan=yes
+ -12.308*marital=divorced + -9.185*marital=married +
-1004.328*marital=single + 8.559*marital=unknown + -11.501*month=apr
+ 9.110*month=aug + -1180.300*month=dec + -189.978*month=jul
+ 14.316*month=jun + -124.764*month=mar + 6203.997*month=may
+ -0.884*month=nov + -9.761*month=oct + 12.301*month=sep +
-990.322*nr.employed + -189.978*pdays + -14.323*poutcome=failure +
4.874*poutcome=nonexistent + -7.191*poutcome=success + 1.698*previous
```

Interpreting the output

The output of the `trainlogistic` command is an equation representing the sum of all predictor variables multiplied by their respective coefficient. The coefficients give the change in the log-odds of the outcome for one unit increase in the corresponding feature or predictor variable.

Odds are represented as the ratio of probabilities, and they express the relative probabilities of occurrence or nonoccurrence of an event. If we take the base 10 logarithm of odds and multiply the results by 10, it gives us the log-odds. Let's take an example to understand it better.

Let's assume that the probability of some event E occurring is 75 percent:

P(E)=75%=75/100=3/4

The probability of E not happening is as follows:

1-P(A)=25%=25/100=1/4

The odds in favor of E occurring are *P(E)/(1-P(E))=3:1* and odds against it would be 1:3. This shows that the event is three times more likely to occur than to not occur.

Log-odds would be 10*log(3).

For example, a unit increase in the age will decrease the log-odds of the client subscribing to a term deposit by 97.148 times, whereas a unit increase in `cons.conf.idx` will increase the log-odds by 1051.996. Here, the change is measured by keeping other variables at the same value.

Testing the model

After the model is trained, it's time to test the model's performance by using a validation set.

Mahout has the `runlogistic` command for the same, the options are as follows:

```
mahout runlogistic --help
```

```
--help              print this list
--quiet             be extra quiet
--auc               print AUC
--scores            print scores
--confusion         print confusion matrix
--input input       where to get training data
--model model       where to get a model
```

We run the following command on the command line:

```
mahout runlogistic --auc --confusion --input train_data/input_bank_data.
csv --model model
```

```
AUC = 0.59
confusion: [[25189.0, 2613.0], [424.0, 606.0]]
entropy: [[NaN, NaN], [-45.3, -7.1]]
```

To get the scores for each instance, we use the `--scores` option as follows:

```
mahout runlogistic --scores --input train_data/input_bank_data.csv
--model model
```

To test the model on the test data, we will pass on the test file created during the split process as follows:

```
mahout runlogistic --auc --confusion --input test_data/input_bank_data.
csv --model model
```

```
AUC = 0.60
confusion: [[10743.0, 1118.0], [192.0, 303.0]]
entropy: [[NaN, NaN], [-45.2, -7.5]]
```

Prediction

Mahout doesn't have an out of the box command line for implementation of logistic regression for prediction of new samples. Note that the new samples for the prediction won't have the target label y, we need to predict that value. There is a way to work around this, though; we can use `mahout runlogistic` for generating a prediction by adding a dummy column as the y target variable and adding some random values. The `runlogistic` command expects the target variable to be present, hence the dummy columns are added. We can then get the predicted score using the `--scores` option.

Adaptive regression model

Mahout has an implementation of meta-learners of `OnlineLogisticRegression`, in which each learner is trained using different learning rates, this implementation is called `AdaptiveLogisticRegression`. By default, it trains 100 regression learners and tosses out learners with lower performance after separating learners that have different learning rates.

Let's look at how to execute `AdaptiveLogisticRegression` using the Mahout command line.

```
mahout trainAdaptiveLogistic --input train_data/input_bank_data.csv
--output model --target y --predictors age job marital education default
housing loan contact month day_of_week duration campaign pdays previous
poutcome emp.var.rate cons.price.idx cons.conf.idx euribor3m nr.employed
--types n w w w w w w w w w n n n n w n n n n n --features 20 --passes
100 --categories 2 --threads 20
```

To validate the model, we will use the `validateAdaptiveLogistic` command. Let's look at the arguments to the command:

```
mahout validateAdaptiveLogistic --help
```

```
--help                          print this list
--quiet                         be extra quiet
--auc                           print AUC
--scores                        print scores
--confusion                     print confusion matrix
--input input                   where to get validate data
--model model                   where to get the trained model
--defaultCategory defaultCategory   the default category value to use
```

We will pass the required parameters to the command and check the output.

```
mahout validateAdaptiveLogistic --input train_data/input_bank_data.csv
--model model --auc --confusion
```

```
AUC = 0.31


==========================================================
Confusion Matrix
----------------------------------------------------------
a       b       <--Classified as
25613   0       |    25613   a     = no
0       3219    |    3219    b     = yes
```

To get the prediction for unseen samples, we have the command line option of `runAdaptiveLogistic`. Using the trained model, we can predict the future by passing the input data. We have `idcolumn` for which Mahout will provide predictions, but again a target variable is required, so we will add a dummy variable again:

```
mahout runAdaptiveLogistic --help
```

```
--help                          print this list
--quiet                         be extra quiet
--input input                   where to get training data
--model model                   where to get the trained model
--output output                 the file path to output scores
--idcolumn idcolumn             the name of the id column for each record
--maxscoreonly                  only output the target label with max scores
```

We need to add an ID column, say a `Client_ID` that represents the ID of each client to the datasets, and then generate predictions.

```
mahout runAdaptiveLogistic --input input_bank_data_client_id.csv --output
result.txt --model model --idcolumn id
```

The output is generated for both classes for each `Client_ID`, with the score representing the probability of belonging to one particular class:

```
Client_ID,target,score
1,yes,0.12908477170604132
1,no,0.8709152282939587
2,yes,0.09414374186718402
2,no,0.905856258132816
3,yes,0.11752872130530191
3,no,0.8824712786946981
4,yes,0.09453376989863829
4,no,0.9054662301013617
5,yes,0.14564154616220942
5,no,0.8543584538377906
```

Code example with logistic regression

Any machine learning algorithm in Mahout requires a few steps.

For classification, the steps are as follows:

1. Read the file, line by line.
2. Encode the features into vectors by splitting the line on the delimiters.
3. If running the MapReduce implementation, convert the vector to the sequence file.
4. Train the model by passing the vector and target variable.
5. Test the model.

Import the `code` folder, which comes with the book into Eclipse or your favorite editor. Go to the package `chapter4.src.logistic` and open the file `OnlineLogisticRegressionTrain.java`.

Train the model

Here, we are reading the file:

```
String inputFile = "data/chapter4/train_data/input_bank_data.csv";
String outputFile = "data/chapter4/logistic/model";
```

We create the predictor list, the names of the column used as predictors:

```
List<String> predictorList =Arrays.asList("age","job","marital","educati
on","default",    "housing","loan","contact","month","day_of_week","dura
tion","campaign","pdays","previous","poutcome",    "emp.var.rate","cons.
price.idx","cons.conf.idx","euribor3m","nr.employed");
```

We encode the feature type; the types are same as shown in the code example, n for numerical and w for categorical variables:

```
List<String> typeList = Arrays.asList("n",  "w",  "w",  "w",  "w",  "w",  "w",
"w",  "w",  "w",  "n",  "n",  "n",  "n","w",  "n",  "n",  "n",  "n",  "n");
```

`LogisticModelParameters` is a helper class, which helps with passing parameters to the `OnlineLogisticRegression` class and returns a `CsvRecordFactory` value with appropriate parameters set. We will look into `LogisticModelParameters` and `CsvRecordFactory` later in the chapter, to help us understand the process better.

Here, we are setting the parameters required by the `OnlineLogisticRegression` class through the `lmp` object of the `LogisticModelParameters` class as follows:

```
LogisticModelParameters lmp = new LogisticModelParameters();
lmp.setTargetVariable("y");
lmp.setMaxTargetCategories(2);
lmp.setNumFeatures(20);
lmp.setUseBias(false);
lmp.setTypeMap(predictorList,typeList);
lmp.setLearningRate(0.5);

int passes = 50;
```

This step creates the appropriate `CsvRecordFactory` object and returns it. The `csv` object will be used to parse and encode the `csv` file into vectors as follows:

```
CsvRecordFactory csv = lmp.getCsvRecordFactory();
```

This step creates the `OnlineLogisticRegression` object by setting the parameters we passed to the `lmp` object as follows:

```
lr = lmp.createRegression();
```

We define `RandomAccessSparseVector` with the size defined by the number of features in the file. We defined it by setting `lmp.setNumFeatures(20)`. `csv.processLine` takes the line read and encodes it into the vector input and returns the target value for that particular instance.

```
Vector input = new RandomAccessSparseVector(lmp.getNumFeatures());
int targetValue = csv.processLine(line, input);
```

At last, we can train the model using the `lr.train` method, which takes the particular instance's target value and the feature vector:

```
lr.train(targetValue, input);
```

The last step is to write the model to a file, so that we can use it later for testing and prediction.

To write the model to the file, we use the `saveTo` function, provided by the `LogisticRegressionParameter` object `lmp`:

```
OutputStream modelOutput = new FileOutputStream(outputFile);
        try {
          lmp.saveTo(modelOutput);
        } finally {
          modelOutput.close();
        }
```

The LogisticRegressionParameter and CsvRecordFactory classes

To work with logistic regression in Java code, Mahout provides a couple of utility classes, `LogisticRegressionParameter` and `CsvRecordFactory`. Let's see how to use them.

A code example without the parameter class

Without using the `LogisticRegressionParameter` class, we can directly construct the `CsvRecordFactory` and `OnlineLogisticRegression` objects as follows. A working version of the code can be found in the `OnlineTrainLogisticExampleWithoutParamater.java` file, in the `chapter4.src.logistic` package:

```
CsvRecordFactory csv = new CsvRecordFactory("y",setTypeMap(predictorList,
typeList)).maxTargetValue(2).includeBiasTerm(false);

lr =new OnlineLogisticRegression(2,20,new L1()).lambda(0).
learningRate(0.5).alpha(1 - 1.0e-3);
```

We have to take care of our own function to write the model as follows:

```java
public static void write(DataOutput out) throws IOException {
    out.writeUTF("y");
    out.writeInt(typeMap.size());
    for (Map.Entry<String,String> entry : typeMap.entrySet()) {
      out.writeUTF(entry.getKey());
      out.writeUTF(entry.getValue());
    }
    out.writeInt(20);
    out.writeBoolean(false);
    out.writeInt(2);

    if (targetCategories == null) {
      out.writeInt(0);
    } else {
      out.writeInt(targetCategories.size());
      for (String category : targetCategories) {
        out.writeUTF(category);
      }
    }
    out.writeDouble(0);
    out.writeDouble(50);
    lr.write(out);
  }
```

Here, we write out all the parameters passed to the `lr` object, so that we can use them later.

Testing the online regression model

Open the `OnlineLogisticRegressionTest.java` code file. To test the model, we will use the test file created from the Mahout `split` command.

```java
private static String inputFile="data/chapter4/test_data/input_bank_data.
csv";
```

```java
private static String modelFile="data/chapter4/model";
```

First, we need to load the model from disk:

```java
LogisticModelParameters lmp = LogisticModelParameters.loadFrom(new
File(modelFile));
```

Read the input file to be tested:

```java
BufferedReader in = OnlineLogisticRegressionTest.open(inputFile);
```

For each line in the file, we encode the features into vectors and then classify each feature set. We also store the actual target value for the row that will be used to derive performance statistics:

```
    Auc collector = new Auc();
while (line != null) {
            Vector v = new SequentialAccessSparseVector(lmp.
getNumFeatures());
            int target = csv.processLine(line, v);
            double score = lr.classifyScalar(v);
            output.printf(Locale.ENGLISH, "%d,%.3f,%.6f%n", target,
score, lr.logLikelihood(target, v));
            collector.add(target, score);
            line = in.readLine();
        }
```

The AUC class is used to derive the confusion matrix and AUC of ROC curve. We pass the predicted values and actual value to the `collector.add()` method.

Logistic regression has other methods for classification, for example, `classify()`, which returns the probability for both classes. I advise you to go through the documentation for further details.

To get the AUC class, use the `collector.auc()` function.

To get the confusion matrix, use the `collector.confusion()` function.

The output of the program:

```
AUC = 0.60
confusion: [[10743.0, 1118.0], [192.0, 303.0]]
entropy: [[NaN, NaN], [-45.2, -7.5]]
```

Getting predictions from OnlineLogisticRegression

Open the `OnlineLogisticRegressionPredict.java` file located in the `chaper4.src.logistic` package in the code repository that comes with this book. The file used for prediction will not have the target variable populated. Most of the steps will be similar to the testing phase and the only difference is that we will not track the performance metrics:

```
private static String inputFile="data/chapter4/input_bank_data_without_
target.csv";
private static String modelFile="data/chapter4/model";private static
String modelFile="data/chapter4/model";
```

The LogisticModelParameters and CsvRecordFactory classes accept an input fie that has a target variable but the target variable will not be present when we perform predictions; so, we will tweak the file to meet the need of predictions. We will change the getCsvRecordFactory() method in LogisticModelParametersPredict and firstLine() in CsvRecordFactory. We rename the files as LogisticModelParametersPredict and CsvRecordFactoryPredict. Ideally, you would either extend the classes or create your implementation; I have renamed the file for ease of explanation.

```
LogisticModelParametersPredict lmp = LogisticModelParametersPredict.
loadFrom(new File(modelFile));
CsvRecordFactoryPredict csv = lmp.getCsvRecordFactory();
OnlineLogisticRegression lr = lmp.createRegression();
```

We modified the firstLine() method so that we don't need to look for the target variable, and changed the signature to accept the target variable name as an argument. getCsvRecordFactory() was modified to return CsvRecordFactoryPredict instead of CsvRecordFactory. CsvRecordFactory has a overloaded method for processLine(), which returns -1 for target variable for new samples.

```
        int target = csv.processLine(line, v,false);
        double score = lr.classifyScalar(v);
```

The score variable will give us the predicted score for each instance.

A CrossFoldLearner example

We have covered all three phases of implementation of a classification algorithm, train, test, and predict. Now, we look at CrossFoldLearner, which does cross-fold validations of log-likelihood and AUC on several OnlineLogisticRegression models. Each record is passed to all but one of the models to train and to the one remaining model to evaluate.

Open the CrossFoldLearnerExample.java file. We will use the cancer.csv file present in the data/chapter4 directory. We have copied the csv to our working directory:

```
BufferedReader br = new BufferedReader(new FileReader("data/chapter4/
cancer.csv"));
```

We open the file to read and ignore the first line.

```
CrossFoldLearner clf = new CrossFoldLearner(5, 2, 10, new L1()).lambda(1
* 1.0e-3).learningRate(50);
```

The parameters passed to the constructor are the number of folds, the number of categories, the number of features, and the prior `L1()` function.

We read the file line by line and split on ",". We then encode the values into vectors and train the `CrossFoldLearner` model as follows:

```
while (line != null) {
if (cnt_line > 0) {
  String[] values = line.split(",");
  double[] vecValues = new double[values.length];

  for (int i = 0; i < values.length - 2; i++) {
  vecValues[i] = Double.parseDouble(values[i]);
        }
int target = Integer.parseInt(values[values.length - 1]);
Vector v = new SequentialAccessSparseVector(values.length);
  v.assign(vecValues);
  clf.train(target, v);


    }
```

After the model has been run, we can either use the `CrossFoldLearner` model or get the individual model. The following is the code to get the information related to AUC and confusion matrix from the individual models:

```
System.out.println("Auc of cross fold learner is "+ clf.auc());
br.close();
int model_number=1;
for (OnlineLogisticRegression model : clf.getModels()) {

lr = model;
br = new BufferedReader(new FileReader("data/chapter4/cancer.csv"));
String pred_line = br.readLine();
int cnt_pred_line = 0;
Auc collector = new Auc();
while (pred_line != null) {
if (cnt_pred_line > 0) {
String[] values = pred_line.split(",");
double[] vecValues = new double[values.length];

for (int i = 0; i < values.length - 2; i++) {
vecValues[i] = Double.parseDouble(values[i]);
}
int target = Integer.parseInt(values[values.length - 1]);
Vector v = new SequentialAccessSparseVector(values.length);
v.assign(vecValues);
```

```
double score = lr.classifyScalar(v);
collector.add(target, score);
}
pred_line = br.readLine();
cnt_pred_line++;

}
br.close();
System.out.println("Auc of model " +model_number+ " = "+ collector.
auc());
Matrix m = collector.confusion();
System.out.println("The confusion matrix is" +m);
model_number++;
}
```

We loop through the model to get individual models, test the individual models, and then compute the respective AUC and confusion matrix.

The `AdaptiveLogisticRegression` algorithm programming paradigm follows a similar flow. I am not going to explain this in great detail; you can look at the code examples for `AdaptiveLogisticRegression` and play with it. Since you already understand the process for `OnlineLogisticRegression`, the code will be pretty straightforward.

Random forest

Random forest introduces us to a category of learning tasks called ensemble learning. In ensemble learning, we train multiple weak learners over the same or different subsets of the dataset. We then combine their outputs to come up with the final answer. It has been empirically proved that an ensemble of weak learners will perform better than any single weak learner, giving the same performance at worst. Random forest is an ensemble learning algorithm with decision trees as the weak learners. It is a very good choice for datasets with missing data values and data with small 'n' or large 'p' problems. By small 'n', we mean a smaller number of rows as compared to a large number of features or 'p'. We will discuss the major features of random forest.

Bagging

Random forest employs bagging. If you recall from *Chapter 2, Core Concepts in Machine Learning*, different samples are created from the training data by randomly selecting rows from the original dataset and replacing them. Decision trees are trained using the different samples of data, and final predictions are done based on taking a majority vote. The algorithm allows users to choose the number of trees to be trained to create a forest.

Random subsets of features

While training different decision trees, a modified tree learning algorithm is employed. For each split in the learning process, a random subset of the features are used. This helps address the issue of training correlated trees; if a few features are highly correlated to the target variable, the majority of the trees will select these features to decide splits. This leads to a large number of correlated trees in the forest. By choosing a random subset, we address the issue of training correlated trees.

Typically, for a dataset with p features, $\lvert \sqrt{p} \rvert$ features are used in each split, though the same can be configured by the user.

Out-of-bag error estimate

Random forest computes an out-of-bag error estimate by constructing different bootstrap samples from the data. The number of bootstrap samples is equal to the number of trees to be created for the random forest model. Each decision tree is constructed by using a different bootstrap sample from the original data. About one-third of the rows are left out of the bootstrap sample and not used in the construction of that particular tree. This is called an out-of-bag sample.

With this approach, each row of data will not be included the training sample of around one-third of the trees, and we will get the prediction of the rows from these trees. For each row or instance in the dataset, we will get a prediction from one-third of the trees during training. If 'A' is the majority predicted class of instance 'X', every time it is out-of-bag, the proportion of time the prediction is not equal to the true class gives us the out-of-bag error estimate. Out-of-bag error estimates gives us a good idea of the model's generalization, even without using a test set.

Studies have shown that the OOB error estimate is as good as the estimate from a separate validation set, so theoretically, we don't need to use a validation set with random forest.

 It is always a good idea to cross-validate your results.

Random forest using the command line

We will use random forest on Hadoop.

```
export MAHOUT_LOCAL=""
```

Next, we will copy the file to HDFS. Random forest implementation doesn't need the header file, which we removed during the training of online logistic regression. Hence, we will use the same input_bank_data.csv file. We don't need to add back the header lines. First, we will create the input directory into which we will copy the file as follows:

```
hadoop fs -mkdir input_bank
hadoop fs -put input_bank_data.csv input_bank
mahout split --input input_bank --trainingOutput train_data --testOutput
test_data -xm sequential --randomSelectionPct 30
```

We need to generate a descriptor file, which will be used by the algorithm to understand the data. Please find the parameters that can be passed to the Describe class, as follows:

```
hadoop jar $MAHOUT_HOME/mahout-core-0.9-job.jar org.apache.mahout.
classifier.df.tools.Describe --help
```

```
Options
  --path (-p) path                          Data path
  --file (-f) file                          Path to generated descriptor
                                            file
  --descriptor (-d) descriptor [descriptor ...]  data descriptor
  --regression (-r)                         Regression Problem
  --help (-h)                               Print out help
```

```
hadoop jar $MAHOUT_HOME/mahout-core-0.9-job.jar org.apache.mahout.
classifier.df.tools.Describe -p train_data/input_bank_data.csv -f
bank_descriptor/bank-additional-full.info -d n 9 c 4 n c 5 n 1
```

Here, we pass the descriptor with the -d option; n stands for numeric or continuous features, c stands for categorical feature, and 1 for label or the target variable.

Let's check the content of the descriptor file, an excerpt from the output is copied as follows:

```
hadoop fs -cat bank_descriptor/bank-additional-full.info
[
  {
    "values": null,
    "label": false,
```

```
      "type": "numerical"
    },
    {
      "values": [
        "entrepreneur",
        "unemployed",
        "services",
        "technician",
        "student",
        "housemaid",
        "blue-collar",
        "retired",
        "unknown",
        "self-employed",
        "management",
        "admin."
      ],
      "label": false,
      "type": "categorical"
    },
    {
      "values": [
        "yes",
        "no"
      ],
      "label": true,
      "type": "categorical"
    }
]
```

For continuous variables, the value is set to `null`, and type set to `numerical`. For categorical variables, the values tag is populated with distinct categories of variables and type set to categorical. The label is set to true only for the target variable. For classification problems, the label is always categorical.

The next step is to train the random forest. First, we will discuss the parameters that can be passed as follows:

```
hadoop jar $MAHOUT_HOME/mahout-examples-0.9-job.jar org.apache.mahout.
classifier.df.mapreduce.BuildForest --help
```

```
--data (-d) path              Data path
--dataset (-ds) dataset       Dataset path
--selection (-sl) m           Optional, Number of variables to select randomly
                              at each tree-node.
                              For classification problem, the default is
                              square root of the number of explanatory
                              variables.
                              For regression problem, the default is 1/3 of
                              the number of explanatory variables.
--no-complete (-nc)           Optional, The tree is not complemented
--minsplit (-ms) minsplit     Optional, The tree-node is not divided, if the
                              branching data size is smaller than this value.
                              The default is 2.
--minprop (-mp) minprop       Optional, The tree-node is not divided, if the
                              proportion of the variance of branching data is
                              smaller than this value.
                              In the case of a regression problem, this value
                              is used. The default is 1/1000(0.001).
--seed (-sd) seed             Optional, seed value used to initialise the
                              Random number generator
--partial (-p)                Optional, use the Partial Data implementation
--nbtrees (-t) nbtrees        Number of trees to grow
--output (-o) path            Output path, will contain the Decision Forest
--help (-h)          _        Print out help
```

Let's now train the model. Here, we are building a random forest with 100 trees, and the feature selection factor is set to 4. The model is written to the final-forest directory, and we can use it to make predictions and evaluate the model.

```
hadoop jar $MAHOUT_HOME/mahout-examples-0.9-job.jar org.apache.mahout.
classifier.df.mapreduce.BuildForest -Dmapred.max.split.size=1874231 -d
train_data/input_bank_data.csv -ds bank_descriptor/bank-additional-full.
info -sl 4 -p -t 100 -o final-forest
```

The next step is to test the performance of the model. To check the parameter options for the class TestForest, please execute the following command:

```
hadoop jar $MAHOUT_HOME/mahout-examples-0.9-job.jar org.apache.mahout.
classifier.df.mapreduce.TestForest --help
```

```
--input (-i) input        Path to job input directory.
--dataset (-ds) dataset   Dataset path
--model (-m) path         Path to the Decision Forest
--output (-o) output      The directory pathname for output.
--analyze (-a)
--mapreduce (-mr)
--help (-h)        _      Print out help
```

Now, let's test the performance on the training data. We pass the location to training data file, the location to the descriptor file, the location to the model, and location to the output directory.

```
hadoop jar $MAHOUT_HOME/mahout-examples-0.9-job.jar org.apache.mahout.
classifier.df.mapreduce.TestForest -i test_data/input_bank_data.csv
-ds bank_descriptor/bank-additional-full.info -m final-forest -a -mr -o
final-pred


========================================================
Summary
--------------------------------------------------------
Correctly Classified Instances          :      26541      92.054%
Incorrectly Classified Instances        :       2291       7.946%
Total Classified Instances              :      28832


========================================================
Confusion Matrix
--------------------------------------------------------
a      b        <--Classified as
1000   2283   |   3283    a    = yes
8      25541  |   25549   b    = no


========================================================
Statistics
--------------------------------------------------------
Kappa                                   0.436
Accuracy                                92.054%
Reliability                             43.4762%
Reliability (standard deviation)        0.5124

hadoop fs -ls final-pred

final-pred/input_bank_data.csv.out

hadoop fs -cat final-pred/input_bank_data.csv.out
```

The output contains the predicted class labels of each row.

To test the performance on the test data, we pass the location to the test data file, the location to the descriptor file, the location to the model file, and location to the output directory.

```
hadoop jar $MAHOUT_HOME/mahout-examples-0.9-job.jar org.apache.mahout.
classifier.df.mapreduce.TestForest -i test_data/input_bank_data.csv
-ds bank_descriptor/bank-additional-full.info -m final-forest -a -mr -o
final-pred_test
```

```
============================================================
Summary
-------------------------------------------------------------
Correctly Classified Instances          :       11079    89.6649%
Incorrectly Classified Instances        :        1277    10.3351%
Total Classified Instances              :       12356


============================================================
Confusion Matrix
-------------------------------------------------------------
a       b       <--Classified as
131     1226    |   1357    a       = yes
51      10948   |   10999   b       = no


============================================================
Statistics
-------------------------------------------------------------
Kappa                                       0.1497
Accuracy                                    89.6649%
Reliability                                 36.3967%
Reliability (standard deviation)            0.5489
```

Predictions from random forest

For prediction, we can follow the same strategy we used for logistic regression and create a dummy target variable. We can get the prediction in the `.csv.out` file in the `final pred` folder.

Naïve Bayes classifier

The naïve Bayes algorithm uses probabilistic learning to make predictions about classes. It is a generative model; it learns the join probability P(X|Y) and then generates conditional probability, using Bayes' theorem. The prefix *naïve* is attributed to this algorithm because the assumptions it makes about the data sound very naïve. The algorithm assumes that the features or predictor variables are all of equal importance and independent of each other. This assumption is rarely true for real-life data. For example, text classification is an area in which naïve Bayes shines, because some words would be more important in predicting the class than others, and some words would be more likely to occur together. In e-mail classification, words like *lottery* or *subscribe* are likely to indicate the message is spam, where the words *lottery* and *won* to occur more frequently. In this example, although both the assumptions of independence and equal importance are wrong, still naïve Bayes performs very well in e-mail classification. The reason for this is still being studied and there are a few papers that try to explain it. However, we won't go into that. The motivation behind the assumptions is computation simplicity, which we will see later.

Let's assume a dataset of 100 e-mails with 20 spams and 80 hams. We want to predict whether an e-mail is ham or spam based on the words in the emails. Without any information about the words in the e-mail, we can guess the probability of an e-mail being spam. It would be 20/100 or 0.2 or 20 percent. This is called **prior probability**. Now, let's suppose that we know that the e-mail has the word Lottery in it. The probability that the word Lottery was used in previous spam e-mails is called **Likelihood**. The probability that the word Lottery was used in any mail, whether spam or ham, is called **marginal likelihood**.

Now, by applying Bayes' theorem for conditional probability, we can compute the probability of an e-mail being spam if it has the word Lottery. This probability is called **posterior probability**.

$$P(spam \mid Lottery) = \Big(P(Lottery \mid spam) * P(spam)\Big) \div P(Lottery)$$

Here, $P(spam \mid Lottery)$ is the posterior probability that we are trying to predict, $\big(P(Lottery \mid spam)\big)$ is the likelihood, $P(Lottery)$ is the marginal probability, and $P(spam)$ is the prior probability.

We will use the frequency table to generate the probabilities as follows:

Frequency	Lottery		Won		Golf		Subscribe		Bank		
	Yes	No	Yes	No	Yes	No	Yes	No	Yes	No	Total
spam	9	11	10	10	0	20	2	18	5	15	20
ham	1	79	10	70	80	0	5	75	9	71	80
Total	1	79	1	79	1	79	1	79	1	79	100

The likelihood table is as follows:

Likelihood	Lottery		Won		Golf		Subscribe		Bank		
	Yes	No	Yes	No	Yes	No	Yes	No	Yes	No	Total
spam	9/20	11/20	10/20	10/20	0/20	20/20	2/20	18/20	5/20	15/20	20
ham	1/80	79/80	10/80	70/80	80/80	0/80	5/80	75/80	9/80	71/80	80
Total	10/100	90/100	20/100	80/100	80/100	20/100	7/100	93/100	14/100	86/100	100

From the likelihood table, we can see that:

$P(Lottery) = 10 / 100 = 0.1$

$(P(Lottery \mid spam)) = 9/20 = 0.45$

$P(spam) = 20/100 = 0.2$

Hence, $P(spam \mid Lottery) = (0.45*0.2)/0.1 = 0.9$

The probability of $P(ham \mid Lottery)$ is 1 - 0.9 = 0.1 as the two events are mutually exclusive. As an exercise, you could derive the probability using the Bayes' theorem. We derived the probability of a particular e-mail belonging to the class spam based on a single feature, but in real-life data there will be multiple features. This is where the assumption of naïve Bayes comes handy. As the features are independent, we can use $P(A \cap B) = P(A)*P(B)$ and generate a simpler formula:

$$P\left(spam \mid f1 \cap \sum f2.. \cap fn\right) = P(f1 \mid spam) * P(f2 \mid spam).. * p(fn \mid spam) * p(spam) \div$$
$$P(f1) * p(f2).. * p(fn)$$

where $fi, i = 1..n$ are the features. From our frequency table, let's assume that the mail contains the words Lottery, Won, and Subscribe, therefore the numerator of the left hand side is 9/20*10/20*2/20*20/100= 0.0045 and denominator is 10/100*20/100*7/100= 0.0014.

Notice in the example table that Golf occurs zero times for spam, so the likelihood of golf is zero too. Now for naïve Bayes, we multiple the probabilities, so for spam the probability is going to be zero if an e-mail contains the word Golf. This is not an ideal scenario, and to address this we add a value, mostly one, to all the frequency counts in the frequency table.

Numeric features with naïve Bayes

As we can see that naïve Bayes uses likelihood based on frequencies, we need the input features to be categorical. To work with numeric features, we need to convert them to categorical features. There are many ways to do this. We can bin the data into categories based on equal weight, or equal widths, or use quartiles, or try to identify natural bins by using the domain expertise about the data.

Command line

We have already seen how to train and test a naïve Bayes classifier by using the Mahout command line in *Chapter 1, Introduction to Mahout*. If you revisit the chapter, you will find that you have a better grasp of the process now.

Summary

In this chapter, we discussed one of the major areas of application in machine learning, known as classification.

We discussed the internal working and learned to use, three of the most popular classification algorithms and discussed all the four processes involved in the classification project: train, test, validate and predict.

In the next chapter, we will discuss topic modeling on top of text data and frequent pattern mining on top of product purchase transactions. Both of the topics have a wide area of practical application and is used extensively by the Industry.

5
Frequent Pattern Mining and Topic Modeling

In this chapter, we are going to discuss two important application areas of machine learning, frequent pattern mining and topic modeling. Frequent pattern mining helps identify frequent patterns among transactions. This type of technique is used widely in market basket analysis, upselling and cross-selling of products, and so on. There are many different algorithms to mine frequent patterns from databases such as Apriori, Tree projection, and FP-Growth; we will restrict our discussion to FP-Growth, which is implemented in Mahout. Topic modeling represents documents under consideration as topics. Each topic is a bag of words that we can use to label the topics. We will also discuss the Mahout implementation of **Latent Dirichlet allocation (LDA)**. The topics covered in this chapter are as follows:

- Frequent pattern mining
- Topic modeling

Frequent pattern mining

FP-Growth represents the frequent transactions in a consolidated data structure called FP Tree, and the frequent patterns are mined using the FP Tree.

There are two major steps while mining frequent patterns using the FP-Growth algorithm, building the FP Tree, and deriving frequent patterns from the FP Tree.

Building FP Tree

Let's assume a database with the following information. For each transaction, we have a list of items that were sold.

Transaction ID	Items
1	Fish, Milk, Egg, Bread, and Biscuit
2	Lemon, Fish, Bread, and Tea
3	Fish and Milk
4	Egg and Tea
5	Fish, Biscuit, Bread, and Cup

Let the minimum support be 2. We first compute the frequency of occurrence of each item in the transaction table. If you are not able to recall what is meant by support, please revisit the section *Frequent pattern mining* in *Chapter 2, Core Concepts in Machine Learning*.

The frequency of occurrence of items is as shown here:

Items	Frequency
Fish	4
Milk	2
Egg	2
Bread	3
Biscuit	2
Lemon	1
Tea	2
Cup	1

Note that support, in this case, is the absolute number and not the percentage coverage.

The next step is to sort the items by their frequencies and drop items lower than the support value of 2. The output of the step is displayed in the following table:

Items	Frequency
Fish	4
Bread	3
Milk	2
Egg	2

Items	Frequency
Biscuit	2
Tea	2

In this step, we reorder the transaction based on respective frequency in descending order. The output of the steps is displayed in the following table:

TransactionID	Items	Reordered
1	Fish, Milk, Egg, Bread, and Biscuit	Fish, Bread, Milk, Egg, and Biscuit
2	Lemon, Fish, Bread, and Tea	Fish, Bread, and Tea
3	Fish and Milk	Fish and Milk
4	Egg and Tea	Egg and Tea
5	Fish, Biscuit, Bread, and Cup	Fish, Bread, and Biscuit

Constructing the tree

The FP Tree has a null root node. So we will start with a null node, add the reordered items of transaction 1, and add the transaction node.

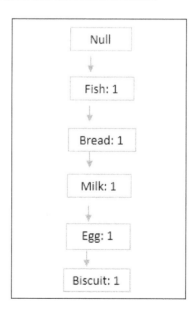

Similarly, we proceed with adding the other transactions and incrementing the count of each element we encounter. As we add transaction 2, we add a node **Tea** after **Bread** and increment the count of **Fish** and **Bread** to 2, and so forth. Note that we require only two scans of the data, the first to collect and sort the list of frequent items and the second to construct the FP Tree. This is one advantage of the FP Tree algorithm compared to other methods such as Apriori.

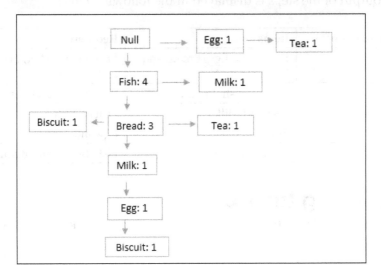

Identifying frequent patterns from FP Tree

The following table shows the item frequency of the FP Tree we had constructed earlier in the chapter:

Items	Frequency
Fish	4
Bread	3
Milk	2
Egg	2
Biscuit	2
Tea	2

To mine the frequent patterns, we go from the bottom to top of this list. We start mining from **Tea** all the way up to **Fish**. First, we create the conditional pattern base for the items under consideration, then we create the conditional frequency, list and lastly create the condition FP Tree.

Let's see how the conditional pattern base for **Tea** is calculated. The steps are listed as follows, in order of they are encountered from fish to tea in each path:

Fish: 1, Bread: 1
Egg: 1

Note that in the conditional pattern base, Tea itself is not present.

The frequency list is given as follows:

Fish: 1, Egg: 1, Bread: 1

The frequent pattern for Tea is as follows:

Fish, Bread: Tea

Egg: Tea

Similarly, we can derive frequent patterns for all other items.

The conditional FP Tree is shown as follows:

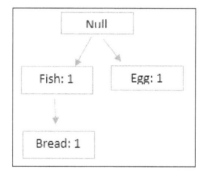

Importing the Mahout source code into Eclipse

It's a good idea to look at the source code of Mahout, as it will give you additional insights into the working of machine learning algorithms and Mahout commands. In this section, we will be exploring and modifying some of the source files of Mahout. For that, we need to import the source code into Eclipse. Mahout source code is packaged in Maven and if all the configuration steps of *Chapter 1, Introduction to Mahout*, were followed, we should be ready to import the source code into Eclipse.

Let's start with downloading the code folder. Please go to the URL `http://archive.` `apache.org/dist/mahout/0.9` and download the file `mahout-distribution-0.9-` `src.tar.gz`. Ideally the file should be copied to the Eclipse workspace directory, but any location can be used. The next step is to extract the archive in the folder where the archive `mahout-distribution-0.9-src.tar.gz` has been copied to. For this, we will execute the following command:

```
tar -xf mahout-distribution-0.9-src.tar.gz
```

This will create the directory `mahout-distribution-0.9`. To import the source into Eclipse, please follow the sequence of steps as follows:

Go to **File** | **Import** | **Maven** | **Existing Maven Projects** | **Next** | Browse to workspace and go to mahout source folder **mahout-distribution-0.9** | **Finish**. Eclipse will download the required dependencies.

Frequent pattern mining with Mahout

So far, we discussed the important concepts needed to understand the frequent pattern mining algorithm and also discussed the construction of a FP Tree with examples. Let's now discuss how to implement **frequent pattern mining** (FPM) with Mahout.

Extending the command line of Mahout

Frequent pattern mining is not currently supported through the Mahout command line. We will learn how to tweak Mahout to support frequent pattern mining from the command line. The approach demonstrated here can be used to support user-created classes from the Mahout command line.

Looking at the source code of the tool you are working with is always a great idea. This gives a strong understanding of the basics and augments the learning process. We will use the Mahout source code imported into Eclipse. Let's open the file `MahoutDriver.java` found in the folder `core/src/main/java/org/apache/` `mahout/driver` under the Mahout directory or from the package `org.apache.` `mahout.driver` in Eclipse. This class is called by the Mahout shell script found in the `bin/` folder. When we run the Mahout command, the `MahoutDriver.java` class is executed. The first argument that we pass to the Mahout script is called the short job name and it maps to a Mahout class to be executed. For example, when we run `mahout trainlogistic`, the class `org.apache.mahout.classifier.sgd.` `TrainLogistic` is executed and the rest of the arguments are passed to the class.

Let's look at these lines in the `MahoutDriver.java` file:

```
Properties mainClasses = loadProperties("driver.classes.props");
  if (mainClasses == null) {
    mainClasses = loadProperties("driver.classes.default.props");
  }
  if (mainClasses == null) {
    throw new IOException("Can't load any properties file?");
  }
```

The code block above is reading the properties file. The mapping of the short job name to the actual class name is maintained in the `properties` file `driver.classes.default.props` present in the `src/conf` or `conf` folder under the `mahout` directory. Let's open the `driver.classes.default.props` file, where we can see that `trainlogistic` is mapped to the class `org.apache.mahout.classifier.sgd.TrainLogistic` as previously mentioned:

org.apache.mahout.classifier.sgd.TrainLogistic = trainlogistic : Train a logistic regression using stochastic gradient descent

There are other `.props` files with the name format `<shortJobName>.props`. These can be used to pass additional parameters to the class to be executed.

Now, to enable Mahout to support frequent pattern mining from the command line, we need to create a class that can perform frequent pattern mining and then add it to the `driver.classes.default.props` file. The Mahout code base already has a Java class to perform the same function in its code base, `org.apache.mahout.fpm.pfpgrowth.FPGrowthDriver`. We will add the following mentioned line in `driver.classes.default.props`. It can be added as a new line anywhere in the file:

org.apache.mahout.fpm.pfpgrowth.FPGrowthDriver = fpg: Frequent Pattern Growth

Additionally, we can create a blank file `fpg.props` although it is not compulsory:

touch fpg.props

Now we can use the command line implementation of frequent pattern mining. Please make sure you have followed the instructions and got the command line for the working of the Mahout FPM, the examples ahead rely on it. Let's see the command line option. Type the following command on the terminal:

mahout fpg --help

The important parameters of the `fpg` job are as follows:

Argument	Description
input (-i) input	This is the path to the job input directory.
output (-o) output	This is the directory pathname for output.
minSupport (-s)	This is the minimum number of times a co-occurrence must be present. The default value is 3.
numGroups (-g)	This is the number of groups the features should be divided into in the MapReduce version. This doesn't work in a sequential version.
splitterPattern (-regex)	This is the regular expression pattern used to split given string transactions into itemsets. The default value splits comma-separated itemsets.
method (-method) method	This is the method of processing sequential | mapreduce.
useFPG2 (-2)	This uses an alternate FPG implementation.

Now we will discuss how to mine frequent patterns and rules using Mahout. The first step is to get the data.

Getting the data

For frequent pattern mining, we will use a dataset with transactions and then try to find out frequent patterns in those transactions. We will use the dataset provided by Dr. Tariq Mahmood, Assistant Professor at the National University of Computer and Emerging Sciences (FAST-NU), Karachi, Pakistan. It is available at `https://sites.google.com/a/nu.edu.pk/tariq-mahmood/`.

The link to the file can be found in the code examples in this book at `https://sites.google.com/a/nu.edu.pk/tariq-mahmood/teaching-1/fall-12---dm/marketbasket.csv?attredirects=0&d=1`.

Data description

This `marketbasket.csv` file contains the list of purchases made in a transaction. An element with the value `true` represents a purchase made, whereas the value `false` represents no purchase for that particular item.

A snippet of the file is as follows:

Basket ID	Hair conditioner	Lemons	Standard coffee
C11867	FALSE	FALSE	TRUE
C5096	FALSE	FALSE	FALSE
C4295	FALSE	TRUE	FALSE
C2837	FALSE	FALSE	FALSE
C2693	FALSE	FALSE	FALSE
C3497	TRUE	FALSE	FALSE
C2696	FALSE	FALSE	FALSE

To use the Mahout frequent mining implementation, we need to preprocess the file to a particular format, with each line representing the items that were purchased in the particular transaction, in this case the **Basket ID**. The items can be delimited and the delimiter can be passed to the `regex` parameter, which defaults to *Tab* or *,*:

```
--splitterPattern (-regex) Default Value: "[ ,\t]*[,|\t] [ ,\t]*"
```

The processed file would look something like this:

```
158
130,230
75
121
213
180
124
4,16,36,42,47,71,97,100,108,117,141,147,186,194,245,269,293
```

Here, each integer represents each item that's been purchased.

We will use Java to convert the file; for larger files, `Pig` can be used to convert the file using `MapReduce`. From the `chapter5.fpm.src` package, open the `CSVToMahoutFormatConverter.Java` file. We will first discuss the code snippet that creates the mapping file:

```
    String data_dir="data/chapter5/";
    String csvFilename = data_dir+"marketbasket.csv";

BufferedReader csvReader = new BufferedReader(new
FileReader(csvFilename));

    String line = csvReader.readLine();
```

```
    String[] tokens = line.split(",");
FileWriter mappingWriter = new FileWriter(data_dir+"item_mapping.csv");
    int itemID = 0;
    for(int idx=1;idx<tokens.length;idx++) {
// loops starts from 1 to ignore the first column // element
mappingWriter.write(tokens[idx].trim() + "," + itemID + "\n");
    itemID++;
    }
    mappingWriter.close();
    csvReader.close();
```

The first line of the file is read to create a `mapping.csv` file, which contains the mapping between the item name and `itemID`. The item name is in the first line itself and we use the column number to generate the `itemID`. We have to ignore the first element of the first line as the Basket ID is not required, hence the first loop starts at `1`.

The second step is to convert the transactions into a Mahout-usable format as described earlier:

```
boolean isfirstLine=true;
    while(true) {
        line = csvReader.readLine();
        if (line == null) {
            break;
        }
        if(isfirstLine)
        {
            //ignore the first line
            isfirstLine=false;
            continue;
        }
        tokens = line.split(",");
        itemID = 0;
        boolean isFirstElement = true;
        for(int idx=1;idx<tokens.length;idx++) {
            if (tokens[idx].trim().equals("true")) {
                if (isFirstElement) {
                    isFirstElement = false;
                } else {
                    datWriter.append(",");
                }
                datWriter.append(Integer.toString(itemID));
            }
```

```
    itemID++;
}
datWriter.append("\n");
```

This code snippet transforms the input file into the required Mahout format. The flag variable `isfirstLine` is used to ignore the header line. For each transaction, wherever we find `true`, we write the column number to the output file. The column number represents the item purchased.

After code execution, you will find two new files created, `item_mapping.csv` and `marketbasket_converted.csv`. The file `item_mapping.csv` holds the mapping item and the corresponding `itemID` that we generated:

item_mapping.csv

```
Hair Conditioner, 0
Lemons, 1
Standard coffee, 2
Frozen Chicken Wings, 3
```

The `marketbasket_converted.csv` file has the item ID of each item purchased for each transaction. This will be used as input for generating the frequent patterns.

marketbasket_converted.csv

```
158
130,230
75
121
213
180
124
```

The next step is to copy the `marketbasket_converted.csv` file to HDFS. First, we create a directory for it:

```
hadoop fs -mkdir fpm
```

Then, we copy the file to this directory:

```
hadoop fs -put marketbasket_converted.csv fpm
```

Now, let's derive the patterns using the command line option we just added in the previous section:

```
mahout fpg -i fpm/marketbasket_converted.csv -o patterns -k 10 -method
mapreduce -s 2
```

The input file is passed with the parameter -i and the output directory with the parameter -o; the method of execution is mapreduce and the minimum support is 2.

We now check the output directory:

```
hadoop fs -ls patterns
Found 4 items
-rw-r--r-- 1 ctiwary supergroup 6098 2014-08-20 23:50 /user/ctiwary/
patterns/fList
drwxr-xr-x - ctiwary supergroup 0 2014-08-20 23:51 /user/ctiwary/
patterns/fpgrowth
drwxr-xr-x - ctiwary supergroup 0 2014-08-20 23:51 /user/ctiwary/
patterns/frequentpatterns
drwxr-xr-x - ctiwary supergroup 0 2014-08-20 23:50 /user/ctiwary/
patterns/parallelcounting
```

The following two files of interest are created in the output directory:

- fList: This is a sequence file with the number of the transaction containing the particular item

- frequentpatterns/part-r-00000: This is a sequence file that contains the frequent patterns for each item

Let's see the result in the fList output file:

```
mahout seqdumper -i patterns/fList


Key: 132: Value: 167
Key: 141: Value: 162
Key: 124: Value: 149
Key: 16: Value: 133
Key: 4: Value: 127
Key: 110: Value: 126
Key: 300: Value: 118
Key: 238: Value: 116
Key: 6: Value: 109
```

The key is the item ID and Value is the number of transactions the item was present in:

```
hadoop fs -ls patterns/frequentpatterns


Found 3 items
-rw-r--r--    1 ctiwary supergroup          0 2014-08-20 23:51 /user/
ctiwary/patterns/frequentpatterns/_SUCCESS
drwxr-xr-x    - ctiwary supergroup          0 2014-08-20 23:51 /user/
ctiwary/patterns/frequentpatterns/_logs
-rw-r--r--    1 ctiwary supergroup      84198 2014-08-20 23:51 /user/
ctiwary/patterns/frequentpatterns/part-r-00000
```

Execute the `seqdumper` command to explore the output:

```
mahout seqdumper -i patterns/frequentpatterns/part-r-00000
```

Let's observe one of the lines of the output:

```
Key: 99: Value: ([99],35), ([16, 99],22), ([141, 99],22), ([132, 99],20),
([141, 16, 99],18), ([132, 16, 99],17), ([132, 141, 99],15), ([132, 141,
16, 99],14), ([132, 124, 99],14), ([132, 141, 124, 16, 99],12)
```

The number `99` of the key represents the `ItemID`, if we check `mapping.csv` it is `Glass Cleaner`. The values represent the top 10 associations of other items with `Glass Cleaner`. `([99],35)` means that `Glass Cleaner` is present 35 times, `([141, 99],22)` represents `White Bread` and `Glass Cleaner` is present 22 times, and so on. All the associations can be looked up in the `mapping.csv` file.

To run in sequential mode, we can pass the argument sequential to the parameter method. Note that in sequential mode, the file needs to be on the file system and not HDFS:

```
mahout fpg -i fpm/marketbasket_converted.csv -o patterns -k 10 -method
sequential -s 2
```

Frequent pattern mining with Mahout API

An example of the Java implementation is in the `FPGrowthExample.Java` class in the package `chapter5.fpm.src`. It has implementations for both sequential and MapReduce execution.

The `run(String[] args, Configuration conf)` function called from the `main` method creates the required parameter object and passes it to the `runPFPGrowth(Parameters params, Configuration conf)` method:

```java
if ("sequential".equalsIgnoreCase(classificationMethod)) {
  System.out.println("Sequential run");
  runFPGrowth(params, conf);
} else if ("mapreduce".equalsIgnoreCase(classificationMethod)) {
  System.out.println("mapreduce run");
  HadoopUtil.delete(conf, outputDir);
  PFPGrowth.runPFPGrowth(params, conf);
}
```

MapReduce execution

The program takes the following input. The input is the same as the one on the Mahout command line:

```
-i fpm/marketbasket_converted.csv -o patterns -k 10 -method mapreduce -s
2
```

The entry part of the parallel execution is the `FPGrowth.runPFPGrowth(params, conf)` function.

We need to call the functions `startParallelFPGrowth(params, conf)` and `startAggregating(params, conf)`:

```
List<Pair<String,Long>> fList = readFList(params);
saveFList(fList, params, conf);

// set param to control group size in MR jobs
int numGroups = params.getInt(NUM_GROUPS, NUM_GROUPS_DEFAULT);
int maxPerGroup = fList.size() / numGroups;
if (fList.size() % numGroups != 0) {
maxPerGroup++;
}
params.set(MAX_PER_GROUP, Integer.toString(maxPerGroup));

startParallelFPGrowth(params, conf);
startAggregating(params, conf);
```

startParallelFPGrowth(params, conf);

The classes used by the `MapReduce` job `startParallelFPGrowth` are given below. The classes are used to set different parameters of the `job` object:

```
job.setInputFormatClass(TextInputFormat.class);
job.setMapperClass(ParallelFPGrowthMapper.class);
job.setCombinerClass(ParallelFPGrowthCombiner.class);
job.setReducerClass(ParallelFPGrowthReducer.class);
job.setOutputFormatClass(SequenceFileOutputFormat.class);
```

startAggregating(params, conf);

The classes used by the `MapReduce` job `startAggregating` are given as follows. The classes are used to set different parameters of the `job` object:

```
job.setInputFormatClass(SequenceFileInputFormat.class);
job.setMapperClass(AggregatorMapper.class);
job.setCombinerClass(AggregatorReducer.class);
```

```
job.setReducerClass(AggregatorReducer.class);
job.setOutputFormatClass(SequenceFileOutputFormat.class);
```

Linear execution

We will next discuss the linear execution of the frequent pattern mining algorithm. The entry point of execution is the function runFPGrowth(params, conf).

The first step is to create the object of the class FPGrowth:

```
FPGrowth<String> fp = new FPGrowth<String>();
fp.generateTopKFrequentPatterns(
new StringRecordIterator(new FileLineIterable(
inputStream, encoding, false), pattern),
fp.generateFList(new StringRecordIterator(
new FileLineIterable(inputStreamAgain,
encoding, false), pattern), minSupport),
minSupport,
maxHeapSize,
features,
new StringOutputConverter(
new SequenceFileOutputCollector<Text, TopKStringPatterns>(
writer)),
new ContextStatusUpdater<Writable, Writable, Writable, Writable>(
null));

List<Pair<String, TopKStringPatterns>> frequentPatterns = FPGrowth
.readFrequentPattern(conf, output);
for (Pair<String, TopKStringPatterns> entry : frequentPatterns) {
log.info("Dumping Patterns for Feature: {} \n{}", entry.getFirst(),
entry.getSecond());
```

Formatting the results and computing metrics

Open the FormatResults.java file present in the chapter5.src package of the code folder that comes with this book, the arguments to be passed are 1361 data/chapter5/item_mapping.csv patterns/fList patterns/frequentpatterns/part-r-00000 0.0 0.0:

```
    int transactionCount = Integer.parseInt(args[0]);
String mappingCsvFilename = args[1];
String frequencyFilename = args[2];
String frequentPatternsFilename = args[3];
double minSupport = Double.parseDouble(args[4]);
double minConfidence = Double.parseDouble(args[5]);

Map<Integer, Long> frequency = readFrequency(configuration,
frequencyFilename);
```

```
Reader frequencyReader = new SequenceFile.Reader(fs,
new Path(fileName), configuration);
Map<Integer, Long> frequency = new HashMap<Integer, Long>();
Text key = new Text();
LongWritable value = new LongWritable();
while(frequencyReader.next(key, value)) {
frequency.put(Integer.parseInt(key.toString()), value.get());
}

readFrequentPatterns(configuration, frequentPatternsFilename,
transactionCount, frequency, itemById, minSupport, minConfidence);

Reader frequentPatternsReader = new SequenceFile.Reader(fs,
new Path(fileName), configuration);
Text key = new Text();
TopKStringPatterns value = new TopKStringPatterns();

double support = (double)occurrence / transactionCount;
double confidence = (double)occurrence / firstFrequencyItem;
double lift = ((double)occurrence * transactionCount) /
(firstFrequencyItem * otherItemOccurrence);
double conviction = (1.0 - (double)otherItemOccurrence /
transactionCount) / (1.0 - confidence);
```

Topic modeling using LDA

The LDA algorithm represents documents under investigation with the help
of multiple topics, where each topic consists of a certain bag of words. LDA
is a generative probabilistic model and makes assumptions made about data
generation. The assumptions made by LDA are as follows:

- There are a fixed number of patterns of word usage, groups of terms that
  tend to occur together in documents and these are called topics.

- Each document is assumed to be formed by the combination of a particular
  set of topics.

For a particular document, the steps are as follows:

1. Based upon Poisson distribution, decide the number of words the document
   will have.

2. For K the number of topics, choose the topic composition for the document.
   For example, 20 percent of topic A, 30 percent of topic B, 30 percent of topic C
   and 20 percent of topic 20.

3. Finally, generate each word, *w*, in the document by:

   1. Picking a topic for the word

   2. Using the selected topic to generate the word itself

Using these steps, the LDA algorithm then tries to backtrack from the documents to find a set of topics that are likely to have generated the document.

With the above mentioned assumptions in place, we proceed to identify the bag of words for each document and assigning each document to a combination of these topics

The next steps are as follows:

1. We go through each document, and randomly assign each word in the document to one of the *K* topics.

2. This random assignment already gives us both the topic representations of all the documents and word distributions of all the topics, but the assignment is arbitrary and we need to improve on this by following these steps:

   1. For each document *d*, go through each word *w* in *d*.

   2. For each topic *t*, we will compute:

   p(topic t | document d) = the proportion of the words in document d that are currently assigned to topic t, and *p(word w | topic t) = the proportion of assignments to topic t over all documents that come from this word w*. Reassign *w* to a new topic, where you choose topic *t* with probability *p(topic t | document d) * p(word w | topic t)*. According to our generative model, this is essentially the probability that topic *t* generated word *w*, so it makes sense that we resample the current word's topic with this probability.

3. In other words, in this step, we're assuming that all topic assignments except for the current word in question are correct, and then updating the assignment of the current word using our model of how documents are generated.

4. After repeating the previous step a large number of times, we will eventually reach a roughly steady state where your assignments are pretty good. So use these assignments to estimate the topic mixtures of each document (by counting the proportion of words assigned to each topic within that document) and the words associated to each topic (by counting the proportion of words assigned to each topic overall).

LDA using the Mahout command line

We will use the Reuters dataset for out topic modeling example. The first step is to download the data and extract it to the working directory, like follows.

On the command line, first set up the working directory as follows:

```
mkdir /tmp/lda
export WORK_DIR=/tmp/lda
```

Then we download the data to a location on the hard drive and extract the downloaded file to the working directory:

```
wget http://kdd.ics.uci.edu/databases/reuters21578/reuters21578.tar.gz
tar xvzf reuters21578.tar.gz -C $WORK_DIR/input
```

We will use the Mahout class `ExtractReuters` to extract the files:

```
mahout org.apache.lucene.benchmark.utils.ExtractReuters $WORK_DIR/input
$WORK_DIR/reutersfinal
```

The next step is to convert the files to the sequence format. We will use the Mahout command `seqdirectory` for that:

```
mahout seqdirectory -i $WORK_DIR/reutersfinal -o $WORK_DIR/sequencefiles/
-c UTF-8 -chunk 5
```

To view one of the sequence files, we will use the `seqdumper` utility:

```
mahout seqdumper -i ./part-m-00000 -o part-m-00000.txt
```

The output is something like this:

```
Input Path: part-m-00000
Key class: class org.apache.hadoop.io.Text Value Class: class org.apache.
hadoop.io.Text
Key: /reut2-000.sgm-301.txt: Value: 2-MAR-1987 04:45:57.78
Key: /reut2-012.sgm-635.txt: Value: 2-APR-1987 12:14:08.24
```

The next step is to convert the sequence file into a term frequency matrix. We will use the Mahout utility `seq2sparse` for that. This matrix can then be used to perform topic modeling:

```
mahout seq2sparse -i $WORK_DIR/sequencefiles/ -o $WORK_DIR/vectors/ -wt tf
```

Mahout has the `cvb` command to perform LDA. The main parameters are as follows:

- The `-i` input folder, where the input files are present
- The `-o` folder, where the output sequence file will be created
- The `-k` parameter is the number of topics to be generated
- The `-x` parameter is the maximum number of words to aggregate into a topic
- The `-ow` parameter instructs Mahout to remove the final output if it exists
- `-dict` tells you where the dictionary is located
- `-dt` is the output path for the document training
- `-mt` is the model topic folder

We execute the Mahout `cvb` command to perform topic modeling on the input dataset:

```
mahout cvb -i $WORK_DIR/reuters-out-matrix/matrix -o $WORK_DIR/reuterslda
-k 20 -ow -x 20 -dict $WORK_DIR/reuters-out-seqdir-sparse-lda/dictionary.
file-* -dt $WORK_DIR/reuters-lda-topics -mt $WORK_DIR/reuters-lda-model
```

To view the results, we will use the Mahout `vectordump` utility:

```
mahout vectordump -i ${WORK_DIR}/reuters-lda-topics/part-m-00000 -o
${WORK_DIR}/reuters-lda/vectordump -vs 10 -p true -d ${WORK_DIR}/reuters-
out-seqdir-sparse-lda/dictionary.file-* -dt sequencefile -sort ${WORK_
DIR}/reuters-lda-topics/part-m-00000
```

The output is stored in the `vectordump` file, to view it, we use the following command:

```
cat ${WORK_DIR}/reuters-lda/vectordump
```

Summary

In this chapter, we discussed two important application areas of machine learning, frequent pattern mining using the FP Growth algorithm, and topic modeling using LDA. These are two very important toolkits for any machine learning practitioner and using these two, many real-life problems can be solved. Both frequent pattern mining and topic modeling are used extensively for exploratory analysis and to gain additional insights.

In the next chapter, we are going to discuss the recommender system built using collaborative filtering. The recommender system is the most popular and mature functionality of Mahout.

6
Recommendation with Mahout

Recommendations are an integral part of our experience on the Internet. Products are recommended to us on an e-commerce site, news items on a news portal, and videos are recommended on sites such as YouTube. There are many different approaches to building a recommender system. In this chapter, we will discuss methods based on collaborative filtering and learn how to implement a recommender system using Mahout. We are going to primarily focus on user-based and item-based recommendation. We will cover the following recommendations:

- User-based recommendation
- Item-based recommendation

Collaborative filtering

Collaborative filtering, generally speaking, is the process of filtering for information or patterns using techniques involving collaboration between multiple data points. Collaborative filtering methods have a wide breadth of applications, ranging from monitoring data such as logs, application on financial data, e-commerce recommendations, and different web applications such as news sites.

In collaborative filtering for recommendation, the underlying assumption is that the best recommendations can be deduced from the interests of similar users. If the interests of two users match for a certain Item then it is highly likely that there interests will match for other items too as compared to another users with no similar interests. The intuition behind collaborative filtering is that people often get the best recommendations from someone with similar tastes like themselves like classmates, colleagues etc.

The primary input for any recommendation system based on collaborative filtering is the past interests of the user, their current browsing history, and a concept of item or user similarity. Collaborative filtering comes in two predominant flavors, user-based recommenders and item-based recommenders. We will discuss them in details in the coming sections.

Similarity measures

Recommender systems are based on the concept of similarity; without the notion of similarity between users or between items, it won't be possible to compute new preferences and recommend items to users. In this section, we will discuss a few important measures implemented in Mahout.

Pearson correlation similarity

The Pearson correlation is a number that indicates the tendency of two series of numbers to increase or decrease together. The range of Pearson correlation is *-1* to *1*, where values close to *1* indicate that the two series change together in the same direction, so they either increase or decrease together. In this case, the two series are considered to be positively correlated. Values close to *-1* indicate negative correlation. The two series change in opposite directions, so if one increases the other decreases. Values close to *0* means that the two series don't have any patterns related to their respective changes.

It won't take a giant leap of imagination to see how the Pearson coefficient can be used for measuring the similarity of users. The preference values of users will be a series of numbers, and we can calculate the Pearson correlation similarity to see which users have a high value of correlation in their preference value. These users will be similar to each other. In Mahout, this similarity measure is implemented as `PearsonCorrelationSimilarity`.

Euclidean distance similarity

The Euclidean distance similarity is based on the distance between users. Users are represented as points in space. Space has as many coordinates as the number of items in the dataset, and the preference value for an item is the coordinate value for the corresponding coordinate. This similarity is implemented in Mahout as `EuclideanDistanceSimilarity`.

The Euclidean distance measure is computed as $1/(1+d)$, where d is the Euclidean distance between two user points. The value is always positive and the range is between *0* and *1*. Values closer to *1* indicate similar users, whereas values closer to *0* indicate users who don't have similar preferences.

Computing similarity without a preference value

Till now, we have seen recommendations with a preference value associated with it. In some scenarios, recommendations could just be an ordered list of items without any preferences or the actual preference value is not important. In these cases, we need similarity measures that work without preference values. We will discuss two of them.

Tanimoto coefficient similarity

Tanimoto or Jaccard coefficient is the ratio count of the number of common items two users have commonly divided by the number of items both the users have preference for. For example, let's assume we have two users A and B.

A has demonstrated preference for items 1, 2, 5, 9.

B has demonstrated preference for items 1, 3, 5, 7, 10.

Count of common items = (1, 5) = 2.

Count of all items with preference = (1, 2, 5, 9, 7, 10, 3) = 7.

Hence, the Tanimoto coefficient is 2/7. It is implemented in Mahout as the class `TanimotoCoefficientSimilarity`.

Log-likelihood similarity

Log-likelihood similarity is similar to Tanimoto coefficient-based similarity, but it additionally calculates how likely it is that the overlap between the two users is due to chance. In a large dataset, users could have common items purely out of chance, and log-likelihood similarity accounts for this. It is implemented in Mahout as a the `LogLikelihoodSimilarity` class.

Evaluating recommender

In *Chapter 2, Core Concepts in Machine Learning*, we discussed concepts to evaluate a recommender system. Here, we will do a quick recap. The recommender can be evaluated using score difference or precision and recall. In score difference, the evaluation is based on the difference between the actual and predicted ratings. Average difference or root mean square are most commonly used. The root mean square evaluation metric is implemented by the `RMSRecommenderEvaluator` class, and the average difference evaluation metric is implemented by the `AverageAbsoluteDifferenceRecommenderEvaluator` class.

Precision and recall is mostly used for Boolean preferences, preferences without a rating value. The implementation for the precision and recall metric is present in the `RecommenderIRStatsEvaluator` class.

We will discuss a few examples of evaluating recommenders in the coming sections.

User-based recommender system

The user-based recommender system is based on the concept of user similarity. The idea behind this algorithm is that similar users share similar preferences. This idea can be leveraged to recommend a new item based on the preference of users that are similar to that of a user for that particular item.

The user-based recommender algorithm works like this. For a given user u, compute the similarity with all other user based on a similarity measure. Shortlist a group of users n, based on a similarity threshold. This group will be called the neighborhood of the user. For every item, I, that u doesn't have a preference for but some users in n have a preference for, compute a weighted average of the preference values. The weighted preference is the product of the similarity of u with a user in n expressing preference for I as the preference value. Adding this weighted preference for all users in n having preference for I gives the weighted sum. Dividing this weighted sum by the number of such users gives the weighted average of preference value p. The value p is the preference for item I for user u, and if this is above a particular threshold, we can recommend the item to u. Similar users are found first, before seeing what those most-similar users are interested in. Only these items become candidates for recommendation for the user u.

To build a user-based recommender, we need preference data, a notion of similarity between users, a notion of neighborhood of users, and a similarity threshold.

User neighborhood

To compute the new item preferences for a user, we need to consider the preferences of users who are similar. A set of users that are similar to the current user are called its neighborhood. In Mahout, the notion of neighborhood is implemented as the `UserNeighborhood` interface. It has two implementations, `NearestNUserNeighborhood` and `ThresholdUserNeighborhood`. We will discuss them in the next section.

Fixed size neighborhood

We could define the neighborhood as N for similar users. Here, the optimum
number of users or optimum size of neighborhood can be determined by
evaluating the recommender with different values. Too small or too large a
value in most cases won't be a good selection. This is implemented in Mahout
as a `NearestNUserNeighborhood` class.

Threshold-based neighborhood

Rather than having a fixed size neighborhood, we could define a neighbor by
threshold. This is particularly helpful as the number of users could vary and hence
the fixed size might be good for one dataset but not for the others. The threshold
value lies between *-1* and *1*. We select a threshold value, say *0.5* and all users with
a similarity of *0.5*, and greater will be considered as neighbors. The similarity
value will be calculated based on the similarity measure selected. Again, there
is no way to determine a good threshold value, and the estimation can be done
only by evaluating the recommender. This is implemented in Mahout as the
`ThresholdUserNeighborhood` class.

The dataset

The dataset used for this chapter is the GroupLens, MovieLens 100K dataset. You
can download the dataset by clicking on `http://files.grouplens.org/datasets/`
`movielens/ml-100k.zip`. The code repository includes one of the files from the
`ua.base` dataset in the directory `chapter6` under the directory `data`. This is a tab-
delimited file with user IDs, item IDs, ratings or preference value, and a time stamp
as the field. In this chapter, the first three fields are of interest. Let's look at some
sample data from the file. User 1 has expressed preference value for items 1 to 10
and the range of preference value is between 1 and 5 as follows:

```
1   1    5   874965758
1   2    3   876893171
1   3    4   878542960
1   4    3   876893119
1   5    3   889751712
1   6    5   887431973
1   7    4   875071561
1   8    1   875072484
1   9    5   878543541
1   10   3   875693118
```

Mahout code example

In this section, we read the input file, create a user-based recommender, and then evaluate the recommender that we build. We also explore a couple of methods related to making recommendation. The building blocks of a user-based recommender in Mahout are as follows:

- A `DataModel` object to represent the preference data
- A `UserSimilarity` object to measure the similarity of users
- A `UserNeigborhood` object to define the neighborhood of users
- A `Recommender` object to build the user-based recommender

Building the recommender

Open the `UserBasedRecommender.java` file from the package `chapter6.src` in Eclipse. To execute the code file from Eclipse, pass the path to the preference file as an argument and hit **Run** from the menu.

The first step is to read the input file described earlier in the text and create a `DataModel` object to represent the file. We use the `FileDataModel` implementation of the `DataModel` super class for representing the file. The dataset used is the same `ua.base` file discussed earlier:

```
File trainingFile = null;
trainingFile = new File(args[0]);
DataModel model = new FileDataModel(trainingFile);
```

Once the data is represented as a `DataModel` object, it's time to create the `UserSimilarity` object using a different similarity implementation class and then define the number of neighbors to consider for a particular user. We will use both fixed size and threshold-based neighborhoods:

```
UserSimilarity pearsonSimilarity = new PearsonCorrelationSimilarity(
model);
UserSimilarity euclideanSimilarity = new EuclideanDistanceSimilarity(
model);
UserSimilarity tanimotoSimilarity = new TanimotoCoefficientSimilarity(
model);
UserSimilarity logLikilihoodSimilarity = new LogLikelihoodSimilarity(
model);
```

The fixed size neighborhood requires a number of neighbors, a similarity object, and the model object as a parameter to the constructor. We create neighborhood objects of all four similarities discussed in this chapter as follows:

```
UserNeighborhood pearsonNeighborhood = new NearestNUserNeighborhood(
1000, pearsonSimilarity, model);
UserNeighborhood euclideanNeighborhood = new NearestNUserNeighborhood(
1000, euclideanSimilarity, model);
UserNeighborhood tanimotoNeighborhood = new NearestNUserNeighborhood(
1000, tanimotoSimilarity, model);
UserNeighborhood logLikilihoodNeighborhood = new
NearestNUserNeighborhood(
1000, logLikilihoodSimilarity, model);
```

The threshold-based neighborhood implementation requires the similarity threshold, a similarity object, and the `model` object as parameter to the constructor. We have set the similarity threshold as `0.1`, which is very low; generally, anything below `0.5` is not a good idea. However, the optimum value of the similarity threshold can only be determined by evaluation. We have created four neighborhood objects using all the four similarities discussed in this chapter as follow:

```
UserNeighborhood pearsonThresNeighborhood = new
ThresholdUserNeighborhood(
0.1, pearsonSimilarity, model);
UserNeighborhood euclideanThresNeighborhood = new
ThresholdUserNeighborhood(
0.1, euclideanSimilarity, model);
UserNeighborhood tanimotoThresNeighborhood = new
ThresholdUserNeighborhood(
0.1, tanimotoSimilarity, model);
UserNeighborhood logLikilihoodThresNeighborhood = new
ThresholdUserNeighborhood(
0.1, logLikilihoodSimilarity, model);
```

The previous steps have created the base objects required for creating the recommenders. Now, we will create the recommenders and use them. I have created a function as we will create multiple recommenders using the different similarity and neighborhood objects that we created so far. The function takes as parameters the model object, the neighborhood object, the similarity object, and a string to denote which similarity measure we are using, and constructs the recommender:

```
private static void performRecommendation(DataModel model,
UserNeighborhood neighbour, UserSimilarity similarity, String Type)
throws TasteException {
Recommender recommender = new GenericUserBasedRecommender(model,
neighbour, similarity);
```

```
long userId = 1;
int numberOfRecommendation = 2;
List<RecommendedItem> recommendations = recommender.recommend(userId,
numberOfRecommendation);

for (RecommendedItem recommendation : recommendations) {
System.out.println("The two recommended item using similarity "
+ Type + "for user " + userId + " is " + recommendation);
}

int userID = 1;
long itemID = 1106;

System.out.println("The estimated prefrence using similarity " + Type
+ "for user " + userId + " is "
+ recommender.estimatePreference(userID, itemID));
}
```

In the function described in the preceeding section, we can see a couple of ways of using the recommender. The `recommend()` function of the recommender object `recommender` takes the user ID as the first argument and returns *n* number of arguments according to the second argument. The values are returned as a list of `RecommendationItem`. We call the recommend function for user ID 1 and get 2 recommendations as follows:

```
long userId = 1;
int numberOfRecommendation = 2;
List<RecommendedItem> recommendations = recommender.recommend(userId,
        numberOfRecommendation);
```

We can print the recommender items and the preference value by looping through the returned object:

```
for (RecommendedItem recommendation : recommendations) {
System.out.println("The two recommended item using similarity "
        + Type + "for user " + userId + " is " + recommendation);
    }
```

The other useful function is `estimatePreference()`. It takes a user ID as the first argument and item ID as the second argument, and gives the preference for the item for the given user ID:

```
int userID = 1;
long itemID = 1106;

System.out.println("The estimated prefrence using similarity " + Type +
"for user " + userId + " is "+ recommender.estimatePreference(userID,
itemID));
```

Finally, we invoke the `recommender` function we defined, with the combination of similarity and user neighborhood objects we created so far. We invoke the function with the respective neighborhood and similarity measure: Pearson Neighborhood is passed with Pearson Similarity and so on. The function will print two recommended items for user 1 and the estimated preference for item 1106 of user 1:

```
performRecommendation(model, pearsonNeighborhood, pearsonSimilarity,
"pearson ");
performRecommendation(model, euclideanNeighborhood,
euclideanSimilarity, "euclidean ");
performRecommendation(model, tanimotoNeighborhood, tanimotoSimilarity,
"tanimoto ");
performRecommendation(model, logLikilihoodNeighborhood,
logLikilihoodSimilarity, "log-likelihood ");

performRecommendation(model, pearsonThresNeighborhood,
pearsonSimilarity, "pearson ");
performRecommendation(model, euclideanThresNeighborhood,
euclideanSimilarity, "euclidean ");
performRecommendation(model, tanimotoThresNeighborhood,
tanimotoSimilarity, "tanimoto ");
performRecommendation(model, logLikilihoodThresNeighborhood,
logLikilihoodSimilarity, "log-likelihood ");
```

The sample output is given later in the text. We can see that the Pearson similarity-based recommender is better at estimating the preference of user 1 for item 1106 than the Euclidean-based recommender. A conclusive best recommender can only be determined by tweaking the values of the neighborhood and evaluating the recommender iteratively. Hence, we will discuss the evaluation of the user-based recommender next:

```
The two recommended item using similarity pearson for user 1 is
RecommendedItem[item:1106, value:5.0]
The two recommended item using similarity pearson for user 1 is
RecommendedItem[item:1026, value:5.0]
The estimated preference using similarity pearson for user 1 is 5.0

The two recommended item using similarity euclidean for user 1 is
RecommendedItem[item:1293, value:5.0]
The two recommended item using similarity euclidean for user 1 is
RecommendedItem[item:1189, value:5.0]
The estimated preference using similarity euclidean for user 1 is
2.9449823
```

Evaluating the recommender

After we have built the recommender, we need to evaluate its performance. Open the `UserBasedRecommendeEvaluation.java` file from the package `chapter6.src`. To execute the code file from Eclipse, pass the path to the preference file as an argument and hit **Run** from the menu.

The first step is to read the preference file in a `DataModel` object. The dataset used is the same `ua.base` file discussed earlier:

```
File trainingFile = null;
trainingFile = new File(args[0]);
DataModel model = new FileDataModel(trainingFile);
```

We then build two objects which will perform evaluation. Score difference based on evaluation using the `AverageAbsoluteDifferenceRecommenderEvaluator` class and precision recall evaluation-based on `GenericRecommenderIRStatsEvaluator`:

```
RecommenderEvaluator scoreBasedEvaluator = new
AverageAbsoluteDifferenceRecommenderEvaluator();
RecommenderIRStatsEvaluator precRecevaluator = new
GenericRecommenderIRStatsEvaluator();
```

Next, we build the different similarity objects as follows:

```
UserSimilarity pearsonSimilarity = new PearsonCorrelationSimilarity(
model);
UserSimilarity euclideanSimilarity = new EuclideanDistanceSimilarity(
model);
UserSimilarity tanimotoSimilarity = new TanimotoCoefficientSimilarity(
model);
UserSimilarity logLikilihoodSimilarity = new LogLikelihoodSimilarity(
model);
```

We also build the neighborhood objects, both fixed sized and threshold-based, using the different similarity object. Sample code lines are shown as follows:

```
UserNeighborhood pearsonNeighborhood = new NearestNUserNeighborhood(
1000, pearsonSimilarity, model);
UserNeighborhood pearsonThresNeighborhood = new
ThresholdUserNeighborhood(
0.1, pearsonSimilarity, model);
```

To perform the evaluation, we define two functions, one for score-based evaluation and the other for precision recall-based evaluation. The score-based function takes the RecommenderEvaluator object, the DataModel object, the UserNeighborhood, and the UserSimilarity object as the parameters. It uses 70 percent of the data for training and 10 percent of the data for evaluation. It then prints the evaluated score. We can run this example multiple times with different neighborhood sizes to determine the optimum size:

```
private static void performEvaluationScoreDiff(
RecommenderEvaluator evaluator, DataModel model,
final UserNeighborhood neighborhood, final UserSimilarity similarity)
throws TasteException {
// Build the same recommender for testing that we did last time:
RecommenderBuilder recommenderBuilder = new RecommenderBuilder() {
public Recommender buildRecommender(DataModel model)
throws TasteException {
return new GenericUserBasedRecommender(model, neighborhood,
similarity);
}
};
// Use 70% of the data to train; test using the other 30%.
double score = evaluator.evaluate(recommenderBuilder, null, model, 0.7,
1.0);
System.out.println("The evaluation score is " + score);
}
```

We call the function with the DataModel object, the RecommenderEvaluator object, and the different UserSimilarity and UserNeigborhood objects we created. Sample calls using the fixed sized neighborhood and threshold-based neighborhood are shown as follows:

```
performEvaluationScoreDiff(scoreBasedEvaluator, model,
pearsonNeighborhood, pearsonSimilarity)
performEvaluationScoreDiff(scoreBasedEvaluator, model,
pearsonThresNeighborhood, pearsonSimilarity);
```

The sample output is given later in the text. We can see that the recommender with a fixed size neighborhood performed slightly better than the threshold-based neighborhood. The optimum option can be determined iteratively by using different fixed size and threshold values, in combination with the different similarities, and selecting the best-performing one:

```
The evaluation score is 0.7279038090804933
The evaluation score is 0.7187479821770454
```

Similarly, we define the evaluator function to perform precision and recall-based evaluation. The function is a bit different from the one used for the score difference evaluator. The evaluator object is now of the `RecommenderIRStatsEvaluator` type, an interface, with the implementation class being `GenericRecommenderIRStatsEvaluator`. The object has methods to get precision and recall:

```
private static void performEvaluationPrecRecall(
RecommenderIRStatsEvaluator evaluator, DataModel model,
final UserNeighborhood neighborhood, final UserSimilarity similarity)
throws TasteException {
RecommenderBuilder recommenderBuilder = new RecommenderBuilder() {
public Recommender buildRecommender(DataModel model)
throws TasteException {
return new GenericUserBasedRecommender(model, neighborhood,
similarity);
}
};
IRStatistics stats = evaluator.evaluate(recommenderBuilder, null,
model, null, 2,
GenericRecommenderIRStatsEvaluator.CHOOSE_THRESHOLD, 1.0);

System.out.println("The precision is " + stats.getPrecision());
System.out.println("The recall is " + stats.getRecall());
}
```

We invoke the function to perform the evaluation, and the sample calls are shown as follows:

```
performEvaluationPrecRecall(precRecevaluator, model,
pearsonNeighborhood, pearsonSimilarity);
```

The sample output is shown later in the text, and the methodology to get the optimum values remains the same. You can try out different values of the parameter and iteratively find the best recommender:

```
The precision is 0.031757754800590836
The recall is 0.028553299492385772
```

Item-based recommender system

Item-based recommendation is based on similarities between items. The idea behind this algorithm is that a user will have a similar preference for similar items.

The item-based algorithm works like this. For every item, *I*, that a user, *u*, has no preference for, compute the similarity between *I* and every other item that *u* has a preference for. Calculate a weighted average, where the weighted preference is the product of similarity of item *I* with any other item that *u* has expressed a preference for with the preference value for that item. Adding this weighted preference for all items that *u* has a preference for gives the weighted sum, and dividing it by the number of such items gives the weighted average of preference value *p*. The *p* value is the preference for item *I* for user *u*, and if this is above a particular threshold, we can recommend the item to *u*.

To build an item-based recommender, we need preference data and a notion of similarity between items.

Mahout code example

In this section, we are going to discuss how to build an item-based recommender using Mahout. The semantics are pretty similar to the user-based recommender. We will build a recommender and then discuss how to evaluate it. The building blocks of an item-based recommender are as follows:

- A DataModel object representing the preference data
- An ItemSimilarity object to measures the similarity of items
- A Recommender object to build the user-based recommender

Building the recommender

The steps to build an item-based recommender are similar to the ones used for a user-based recommender. Instead of a `UserSimilarity` object, we will use `ItemSimilarity` for building the recommender.

Open the `ItemBasedRecommender.java` file from the package `chapter6.src`. To execute the code file from Eclipse, pass the path to the preference file as an argument and hit **Run** from the menu.

The first step is to represent the preference file, discussed earlier, in a `DataModel` object. The dataset used is the same `ua.base` file discussed earlier:

```
File trainingFile = null;
trainingFile = new File(args[0]);
DataModel model = new FileDataModel(trainingFile);
```

The second step is to create the different similarity objects:

```
ItemSimilarity pearsonSimilarity = new PearsonCorrelationSimilarity(
model);
ItemSimilarity euclideanSimilarity = new EuclideanDistanceSimilarity(
model);
ItemSimilarity tanimotoSimilarity = new TanimotoCoefficientSimilarity(
model);
ItemSimilarity logLikilihoodSimilarity = new LogLikelihoodSimilarity(
model);
```

Once the similarity objects have been created, the next step is to create the `Recommender` object. To do this, we have defined a `performItemRecommendation()` function. The function accepts as arguments the `DataModel` object, the `ItemSimilarity` object, and a string to denote the type of similarity used:

```
private static void performItemRecommendation(DataModel model,
ItemSimilarity itemSimilarity, String Type) throws TasteException {
long userId = 1;
int numberOfRecommendation = 2;


Recommender itemRecommender = new GenericItemBasedRecommender(model,
itemSimilarity);


List<RecommendedItem> itemBasedRecommendations = itemRecommender
.recommend(userId, numberOfRecommendation);


for (RecommendedItem recommendation : itemBasedRecommendations) {
System.out.println("The two recommended item using similarity "
+ Type + "for user " + userId + " is " + recommendation);
}


int userID = 1;
long itemID = 1106;


System.out.println("The estimated prefrence using similarity " + Type
+ "for user " + userId + " is "
+ itemRecommender.estimatePreference(userID, itemID));
}
```

The function fetches the recommended items for user 1. The function that used `recommend()` is the same one that is used in the user-based recommender example, as follows:

```
long userId = 1;
int numberOfRecommendation = 2;
List<RecommendedItem> itemBasedRecommendations = itemRecommender.
recommend(userId, numberOfRecommendation);
```

Once the recommendations are available, we can get the recommended items for the particular user by looping through the list of `RecommendedItem`:

```
for (RecommendedItem recommendation : itemBasedRecommendations) {
    System.out.println(recommendation);
    }
```

The function also uses the `estimatePreference()` method of the `Recommender` object `itemRecommender` to get the preference of a user for an item as follows:

```
int userID = 1;
long itemID = 1106;
System.out.println(itemRecommender.estimatePreference(userID,itemID));
```

Next, we call the function and observe the output. The sample call to the function and partial output is shown as follows:

```
performItemRecommendation(model, pearsonSimilarity, "pearson ");
performItemRecommendation(model, euclideanSimilarity, "euclidean ");
```

```
The two recommended item using similarity pearson for user 1 is
RecommendedItem[item:345, value:5.0]
The two recommended item using similarity pearson for user 1 is
RecommendedItem[item:320, value:5.0]
The estimated prefrence using similarity pearson for user 1 is 4.180895
The two recommended item using similarity euclidean for user 1 is
RecommendedItem[item:1653, value:4.509804]
The two recommended item using similarity euclidean for user 1 is
RecommendedItem[item:1156, value:4.3728814]
The estimated prefrence using similarity euclidean for user 1 is
3.7780771
```

Evaluating the recommender

Open the `ItemBasedRecommenderEvaluation.java` file from the package `chapter6.src`. This code file has the sample code for evaluating an item-based recommender. To execute the code file from Eclipse, pass the path to the preference file as an argument and hit **Run** from the menu.

First, we represent the preference file as a `DataModel` object using the `FileDataModel` class. The dataset used is the same `ua.base` file discussed earlier:

```
File trainingFile = null;
trainingFile = new File(args[0]);
DataModel model = new FileDataModel(trainingFile);
```

We then build the two objects the will perform the evaluation. Score difference-based evaluation using the `AverageAbsoluteDifferenceRecommenderEvaluator` class and precision recall-based evaluation based on `GenericRecommenderIRStatsEvaluator`:

```
RecommenderEvaluator scoreBasedEvaluator = new
AverageAbsoluteDifferenceRecommenderEvaluator();
RecommenderIRStatsEvaluator precRecevaluator = new
GenericRecommenderIRStatsEvaluator();
```

Next, we build the different similarity objects:

```
ItemSimilarity pearsonSimilarity = new PearsonCorrelationSimilarity(
model);
ItemSimilarity euclideanSimilarity = new EuclideanDistanceSimilarity(
model);
ItemSimilarity tanimotoSimilarity = new TanimotoCoefficientSimilarity(
model);
ItemSimilarity logLikilihoodSimilarity = new LogLikelihoodSimilarity(
model);
```

To perform the evaluation, we define two functions, one for score-based evaluation and the other for precision recall-based evaluation. The score-based function takes the `RecommenderEvaluator` object, the `DataModel` object and the `ItemSimilarity` object as the parameters. It uses 70 percent of the data for training and 10 percent of the data for evaluation. It then prints the evaluated score:

```
private static void performEvaluationScoreDiff(
RecommenderEvaluator evaluator, DataModel model,
final ItemSimilarity itemSimilarity) throws TasteException {
// Build the same recommender for testing that we did last time:
```

```
RecommenderBuilder recommenderBuilder = new RecommenderBuilder() {
public Recommender buildRecommender(DataModel model)
throws TasteException {
return new GenericItemBasedRecommender(model, itemSimilarity);
}
};
// Use 70% of the data to train; test using the other 30%.
double score = evaluator.evaluate(recommenderBuilder, null, model, 0.7,
1.0);
System.out.println("The evaluation score is " + score);
}
```

We call the function with the `DataModel` object, the `RecommenderEvaluator`
object, and the different `ItemSimilarity` objects we created. Sample calls are
shown as follows:

```
performEvaluationScoreDiff(scoreBasedEvaluator, model,
pearsonSimilarity);
performEvaluationScoreDiff(scoreBasedEvaluator, model,
euclideanSimilarity);
```

The sample output is given later in the text. We can see that recommender
with Euclidean similarity has performed better than that with Pearson similarity.
The optimum option can be determined by selecting the recommender with the
highest score:

```
The evaluation score is 0.6664933304675151
The evaluation score is 0.7998527691989347
```

Similarly, we define the evaluator function to perform precision and
recall-based evaluation. The function is a bit different from the one
used for score difference evaluator. The evaluator object is now of the
`RecommenderIRStatsEvaluator` type, an interface, with the implementation
class being `GenericRecommenderIRStatsEvaluator`. The object has methods
to get precision and recall:

```
private static void performEvaluationPrecRecall(
RecommenderIRStatsEvaluator evaluator, DataModel model,
final ItemSimilarity itemSimilarity) throws TasteException {
RecommenderBuilder recommenderBuilder = new RecommenderBuilder() {
public Recommender buildRecommender(DataModel model)
throws TasteException {
return new GenericItemBasedRecommender(model, itemSimilarity);
}
};
```

```
IRStatistics stats = evaluator.evaluate(recommenderBuilder, null,
model, null, 2,
GenericRecommenderIRStatsEvaluator.CHOOSE_THRESHOLD, 1.0);

System.out.println("The precision is " + stats.getPrecision());
System.out.println("The recall is " + stats.getRecall());
}
```

We invoke the function to perform the evaluation. Sample calls are shown as follows:

```
performEvaluationPrecRecall(precRecevaluator, model, pearsonSimilarity)
```

The sample output is shown, and the methodology to get the optimum values remain the same:

```
The precision is 0.0012690355329949235
The recall is 0.0012690355329949235
```

Inferring preferences

Sparse datasets with users providing preferences for only a fraction of the items are problematic. As users have provided preferences for only a few items, it will be difficult to generate meaningful preferences. One way to address this scenario is to impute or infer the missing preferences for user-item pairs. Mahout has an implementation for this as the AveragingPreferenceInferrer class, which extends the PreferenceInferrer interface. This implementation computes the average of all preferences provided by a user and imputes the average for all the missing item preferences for that user.

Summary

In this chapter, we learned about the basics of building a recommender system using Mahout. We discussed the idea behind recommender systems, similarity measures, and two paradigms for building the recommender, user-based and item-based. We also discussed a couple of use cases for building a recommender and learned how to measure the efficacy of a recommender system.

In the next chapter, we are going to look at clustering algorithms. We will look at the basic concepts of different clustering algorithms and discuss practical examples.

7
Clustering with Mahout

In this chapter, we will discuss one of the major application areas of machine learning. Cluster analysis has wide areas of application like customer segmentation, news grouping, grouping users based on their behavior, and so on.

We will also get an understanding of the internals of a few important clustering algorithms and then discuss their implementation in Mahout. The topics that we will discuss in this chapter are as follows:

- Data preprocessing
- k-means
- Canopy clustering
- Fuzzy k-means
- Streaming k-means

k-means

k-means is one of the simplest and most widely-used clustering algorithms. Given the number of K clusters to look for, k-means provides K clusters with respective data points belonging to a cluster, depending upon how close they are to the mean of that particular cluster mean. The point is assigned to a cluster to whose mean it is the closest. In other words, k-means tries to minimize the variance between points belonging to the same cluster. The algorithm requires one major input to look for the number of clusters, which can be both a bane and boon. We will discuss this further in this chapter. The other parameters that can be set are the distance measure to be used, the stopping criteria, the number of iterations, and so on. There are two steps in this algorithm.

In the first step we find the points that are nearest to each centroid point and assigns them to that specific cluster. In the second step we recalculate the centroid point using the mean of the coordinates of all the points in that cluster. These steps are repeated till the algorithm converges based on the stopping criteria or the maximum number of iterations. The stopping criteria for k-means is when the centroid doesn't change by a certain degree between iterations or there is no reallocation of points. If the stopping criteria is not achieved, then the algorithm breaks after a certain number of iterations fixed by the user. The choice of the distance measure is governed by the problem at hand. The objective of k-means is to decrease the variance of individual clusters and increase the variance between clusters. As variance is defined under `EuclideanDistanceMeasure`, it is the preferred choice for a distance measure. For text mining, the preferred distance measure is `CosineDistanceMeasure`. An important advantage is that it can account for documents of different sizes.

> k-means is based on variance minimization around the mean. The variance and mean are well defined in the case of the Euclidean distance measure and hence it is recommended to use the Euclidean distance measure with k-means.

Let's look at an example to understand k-means better. Let's assume a dataset with two input features A and B. We intend to cluster them with K. The number of the cluster is set to 2.

The following table shows the first seven lines of the input data:

Input	A	B
1	1.0	1.0
2	1.5	2.0
3	3.0	4.0
4	5.0	7.0
5	3.5	5.0
6	4.5	5.0
7	3.5	4.5

We start with the initial centers; in this case, we assign the farthest point as the initial cluster mean. There are many approaches to determining the initial cluster mean, and we will discuss them shortly.

	Individual	Mean Vector (centroid)
Centre 1	1	(1.0, 1.0)

	Individual	Mean Vector (centroid)
Centre 2	4	(5.0, 7.0)

The input points are now assigned to the respective cluster based on the shortest Euclidean distance from the cluster mean. After the addition of each input point, the centers are recalculated:

Step	Cluster 1		Cluster 2	
	Points	Mean Vector (centroid)	Points	Mean Vector (centroid)
1	1	(1.0, 1.0)	4	(5.0, 7.0)
2	1, 2	(1.2, 1.5)	4	(5.0, 7.0)
3	1, 2, 3	(1.8, 2.3)	4	(5.0, 7.0)
4	1, 2, 3	(1.8, 2.3)	4, 5	(4.2, 6.0)
5	1, 2, 3	(1.8, 2.3)	4, 5, 6	(4.3, 5.7)
6	1, 2, 3	(1.8, 2.3)	4, 5, 6, 7	(4.1, 5.4)

After the first pass of data, we are left with two clusters with points 1,2,3 belonging to cluster 1 with centroid (1.8,2.3) and 4,5,6,7 belonging to cluster 2 with centroid (4.1, 5.4), respectively.

	Points	Mean Vector (centroid)
Cluster 1	1, 2, 3	(1.8, 2.3)
Cluster 2	4, 5, 6, 7	(4.1, 5.4)

In the next iteration, we compare each point's distance to its own cluster mean and to that of the opposite cluster. The Euclidean distance measure is again used to calculate the distance. We observe that point 3 is nearer to cluster 2's mean than cluster 1's mean. Point 3 needs to be reassigned to cluster 2:

Points	Distance to mean (centroid) of Cluster 1	Distance to mean (centroid) of Cluster 2
1	1.5	5.4
2	0.4	4.3
3	2.1	1.8
4	5.7	1.8
5	3.2	0.7

Points	Distance to mean (centroid) of Cluster 1	Distance to mean (centroid) of Cluster 2
6	3.8	0.6
7	2.8	1.1

After the reassignment of point 3, the cluster mean needs to be recalculated again:

	Points	Mean Vector (centroid)
Cluster 1	1, 2	(1.3, 1.5)
Cluster 2	3, 4, 5, 6, 7	(3.9, 5.1)

The iterative relocation continues from this new partition until no more relocations occur or the change in the mean between the iterations is below a certain threshold. If none of the conditions are met, the algorithm should break after a fixed number of iterations.

Deciding the number of clusters

There is no simple way to decide the number of clusters to generate. It depends on the data and the problem to be solved. The good news is that often the problem statement itself leads to the number of clusters. For example, let's assume we want to cluster users based on the product usage; intuitively clusters of high, medium, and low usage make sense. So, based on our intuition of 3 clusters, we can also generate clusters around the neighborhood of numbers like 2, 4, and 5 and select the best one depending on the cluster evaluation metric. Please note that business users don't need the best clusters, they need actionable clusters.

Another rule of thumb is to take the square root of the number of data points divided by 2;

$$k <= \sqrt{\frac{n}{2}}$$

We can also run some algorithms to determine the number of K from the data itself. Most tools have such utilities. In Mahout, we have canopy clustering for this. We will discuss canopy clustering later in this chapter.

Deciding the initial centroid

The choice of the initial centroid impacts the convergence of the clusters and to an extent the quality of the clusters as well. It is important to understand the various choices of deciding the initial centroids and applying at least a couple of these techniques while building the clusters. Let's look at the major techniques.

Random points

One approach to initialize the centroids is to generate random points to represent the centroids equal to the number of the cluster K. The final output will vary depending on the initial points generated, but still this is a viable approach as the output in majority of cases vary by a small margin.

Points from the dataset

The second approach is to select random input points to represent the centroids equal to the number of the cluster K. This approach is similar to the first approach.

Partition by range

In the third approach, we take the range of the individual column, divide it into equal-spaced partitions, and use the partition points as the initial centroids. This approach might lead to a faster convergence of the algorithm.

Canopy centroids

Another possibility is to use the centroids generated by canopy clustering. This is one of the optimum approaches of selecting the centroids and providing both a suitable number of K and good initial cluster points.

If it is possible to run the clustering algorithm multiple times, that is, if we have enough time and resources, the optimum solution is to build different models using all the techniques of deciding initial centroids discussed previously. Once all the k-means converge, we can calculate the average of all the centroids created, use it as the new initial centroid, and run a final iteration of k-means. This final k-means model should determine the final clusters.

Advantages and disadvantages

Like any machine learning algorithms, k-means has its advantages and disadvantages.

The advantages are that k-means is very fast and provides intuitive understanding. Given that we have a good approximation of K, the algorithm provides pretty robust clusters, which is dependent on a close approximation of K. Assumption of spherical clusters might not be good for more complex datasets. The output is dependent on the initial centroid points.

Canopy clustering

Canopy clustering is a fast and approximate clustering technique. It divides the input data points into overlapping clusters called canopies. Two different distance thresholds are used for the estimation of the cluster centroids. Canopy clustering can provide a quick approximation of the number of clusters and initial cluster centroids of a given dataset. It is mainly used to understand the data and provide input to algorithms such as k-means.

 Overlapping clustering algorithms group points into different clusters without the condition of exclusivity of points. A single point can belong to different clusters.

Canopy clustering creates clusters with a single pass over the data. By running canopy clustering algorithm on a dataset we can quickly get an estimate of the number of clusters in the dataset.

The algorithm uses a fast distance measure and two distance thresholds to compute the clusters, the distance measures are Tl and T2, with Tl> T2. For each iteration each point in the dataset is picked and added to a canopy with the point as the centre, then distances from each canopy centre is calculated, if the distance is within T1 then the point is added to the canopy if it is greater than T2 then a new canopy is formed with the point and if the distance is between T1 and T2 then the point is removed.

This threshold between T1 and T2 prevents points close to an existing canopy from forming a close similar and redundant canopy. With this approach we get a pretty good estimate of the number of clusters in the dataset.

Fuzzy k-means

Fuzzy k-means clustering is similar to k-means clustering but unlike k-means the clusters can be overlapping. A single point can belong to more than 1 cluster. Fuzzy k-means we need to estimate the number of clusters k and additionally the fuzziness factor m.

Deciding the fuzzy factor

The fuzziness factor determines the degree of overlap in the clusters. If the fuzziness factor is 1 then fuzzy k-means behaves like k-means, as the fuzziness factor increases we see increased overlap in the clusters.

A Mahout command-line example

Now, we will discuss how to cluster objects using the Mahout command line. We start with getting the data first.

Getting the data

We will use the seed dataset from our favorite UCI repository for clustering examples. The dataset is available at `https://archive.ics.uci.edu/ml/datasets/seeds`.

To download the data, we can execute the following command:

```
wget https://archive.ics.uci.edu/ml/machine-learning-databases/00236/
seeds_dataset.txt
```

We also have the data downloaded in `data/chapter7` in our code base.

Data description

The seed dataset consists of 8 attributes as follows:

Column	Data type
Area (A)	Continuous
Perimeter (P)	Continuous
Compactness (C = 4*pi*A/P^2)	Continuous
Length of kernel	Continuous
Width of kernel	Continuous
Asymmetry coefficient	Continuous
Length of kernel groove	Continuous
Type of seed	Categorical

We can use all the columns for our clustering example or keep *Type of seed* as an external evaluation metric.

Sample data

15.26 14.84 0.871 5.763 3.312 2.221 5.22 1

14.88 14.57 0.8811 5.554 3.333 1.018 4.956 1

14.29 14.09 0.905 5.291 3.337 2.699 4.825 1

13.84 13.94 0.8955 5.324 3.379 2.259 4.805 1

16.14 14.99 0.9034 5.658 3.562 1.355 5.175 1

Preprocessing the data

The first step of preprocessing is to clean the data file. In this particular case, the delimited file has an extra character as a delimiter in a few lines. You can use your favorite text editor to clean it or use the cleaned file in the data directory of the code base. The next step is to convert the file into vectors and save it in the sequence file.

Before we convert the text in file into vectors, we need to clean the file and copy it to HDFS. Navigate to the directory `learningApacheMahout/data/chapter7`. We need to create a directory on HDFS to keep the data file, please execute the following command on the command prompt. This will create the input directories:

```
hadoop fs -mkdir chapter7/clustering_input
```

We need to remove extra characters from the delimiter of the data file `seeds_dataset.txt`, we will use the `sed` for that, please execute the following command on the command prompt:

```
sed -ie "s/[[:space:]]\+/ /g" seeds_dataset.txt
```

Now we need to copy the cleaned file into the HDFS directory `chapter7/clustering_input`, please execute the following command on the command prompt:

```
hadoop fs -put seeds_dataset.txt chapter7/clustering_input/
```

From the code example, open the Java `DataPreprocessing.Java` file. This file is located in the `chapter7.src` package. We first create the `Configuration` object, set the required resources, and then pass the `Configuration` object to `FileSystem`:

```
Configuration conf = new Configuration();
conf.addResource(new Path("/usr/local/hadoop/conf/core-site.xml"));
conf.addResource(new Path("/usr/local/hadoop/conf/hdfs-site.xml"));

FileSystemfileSystem = FileSystem.get(conf);
```

We then create the input and output `Path` objects:

```
String inputPath="chapter7/clustering_input";
String inputSeq="clustering_seq";

Path inputDir = new Path(inputPath);
Path inputSeqDir = new Path(inputSeq);
```

The last step is to use the `InputDriver` class to create the sequence file. `InputDriver` is a utility class in Mahout to convert the tab-delimited file into the sequence file.

Apart from the input and output directory, it takes the vector class name; in this case, `org.apache.mahout.math.RandomAccessSparseVector` and the `Configuration` object:

```
InputDriver.runJob(inputDir, inputSeqDir,          "org.apache.mahout.
math.RandomAccessSparseVector",conf);
```

We take a look at the following output directory:

```
hadoop fs -ls clustering_output
/user/ctiwary/clustering_seq/_SUCCESS
/user/ctiwary/clustering_seq/part-m-00000
```

The sequence file is written to the `clustering_seq/part-m-00000` file. To look at the contents of this file, we will use the `mahout seqdumper` command-line utility:

```
mahout seqdumper -i clustering_seq/part-m-00000

Key: 8: Value: {0:12.37,2:0.8567,1:13.47,5:3.919,3:5.204,7:3.0,6:5.001,4:
2.96}
Key: 8: Value: {0:12.19,2:0.8783,1:13.2,5:3.631,3:5.137,7:3.0,6:4.87,4:2.
981}
Key: 8: Value: {0:11.23,2:0.8511,1:12.88,5:4.325,3:5.14,7:3.0,6:5.003,4:2
.795}
Key: 8: Value: {0:13.2,2:0.8883,1:13.66,5:8.315,3:5.236,7:3.0,6:5.056,4:3
.232}
Key: 8: Value: {0:11.84,2:0.8521,1:13.21,5:3.598,3:5.175,7:3.0,6:5.044,4:
2.836}
Key: 8: Value: {0:12.3,2:0.8684,1:13.34,5:5.637,3:5.243,7:3.0,6:5.063,4:2
.974}
```

k-means

Let's start with checking the command-line options. We will describe some of the most commonly-used parameters.

The command-line options are as follows:

Parameters	Description
`--input (-i)`	Path to input directory
`--output (-o)`	Path to output directory
`--distanceMeasure (-dm)`	The class name given to the distance measure to be used
`--clusters (-c)`	The input centroid as vectors in the sequence format
`--numClusters (-k)`	The number of clusters to be generated
`--convergenceDelta (-cd)`	The convergence delta value
`--maxIter (-x)`	The maximum number of iterations to be performed
`--overwrite (-ow)`	Overwrite the input directory if it is present
`--clustering (-cl)`	If present, perform clustering after the convergence of the centroid
`--method (-xm)`	Sequential or MapReduce execution

From the data preprocessing step, we converted the input file into sequence file format that can be used by Mahout. We pass the sequence file as the input directory using the -i parameter option as follows:

```
mahout kmeans -i clustering_seq -c kmeans_init_cluster -o clustering_
output -dmorg.apache.mahout.common.distance.EuclideanDistanceMeasure -x
10 -k
```

The Mahout k-means command line creates the initial cluster points. It takes the first approach that we described to create k number of random points passed with the parameter -k. We pass the command, the distance measure to use, the output clustering directory, the max number of iterations, and the path to the input dataset.

After we run the algorithm, let's investigate the output directory:

```
hadoop fs -ls clustering_output
```

The output is given as follows:

```
/user/ctiwary/clustering_output/_policy
/user/ctiwary/clustering_output/clusteredPoints
/user/ctiwary/clustering_output/clusters-0
/user/ctiwary/clustering_output/clusters-1
/user/ctiwary/clustering_output/clusters-2
/user/ctiwary/clustering_output/clusters-3-final
```

Files in the folder have the mapping of the vector to clusterclustering_output/clusteredPoints/.

The final cluster of the centroids is present in the clusters-*-final directory. Here the star can be replaced by the number of clusters passed.

We will use Mahout's clusterdump utility to view the clustering output:

```
mahout clusterdump -i clustering_output/clusters-3-final/part-r-00000
```

An excerpt of the output is copied later in text. In this output, each line represents a cluster. The number after VL represents the cluster label, the vector with c represents the centroid as follows:

```
VL-198{n=71 c=[14.120, 14.201, 0.878, 5.476, 3.214, 2.603, 5.081, 1.169]
r=[1.143, 0.565, 0.017, 0.236, 0.165, 1.024, 0.275, 0.503]}
VL-79{n=72 c=[18.329, 16.124, 0.885, 6.142, 3.683, 3.602, 5.994, 1.917]
r=[1.367, 0.600, 0.015, 0.263, 0.168, 1.213, 0.284, 0.276]}
VL-180{n=67 c=[11.876, 13.257, 0.848, 5.238, 2.850, 4.968, 5.124, 2.970]
r=[0.775, 0.361, 0.021, 0.135, 0.151, 1.210, 0.154, 0.243]}
```

Now, we will use the `seqdumper` utility to view the data point to cluster mapping. The key is the cluster label. We have the distance from the cluster centroid and the vector:

```
mahout seqdumper -i clustering_output/clusteredPoints
```

```
Key: 180: Value: wt: 1.0 distance: 1.4086324273887754  vec: 8 = [12.190,
13.200, 0.878, 5.137, 2.981, 3.631, 4.870, 3.000]
Key: 180: Value: wt: 1.0 distance: 1.0009021862979366  vec: 8 = [11.230,
12.880, 0.851, 5.140, 2.795, 4.325, 5.003, 3.000]
Key: 180: Value: wt: 1.0 distance: 3.6425075218638305  vec: 8 = [13.200,
13.660, 0.888, 5.236, 3.232, 8.315, 5.056, 3.000]
Key: 180: Value: wt: 1.0 distance: 1.375878190644538  vec: 8 = [11.840,
13.210, 0.852, 5.175, 2.836, 3.598, 5.044, 3.000]
Key: 180: Value: wt: 1.0 distance: 0.808719839391573  vec: 8 = [12.300,
13.340, 0.868, 5.243, 2.974, 5.637, 5.063, 3.000]
Key: 79: Value: wt: 1.0 distance: 0.8256480988955742  vec: 8 = [18.300,
15.890, 0.911, 5.979, 3.755, 2.837, 5.962, 2.000]
Key: 79: Value: wt: 1.0 distance: 0.9602824919371283  vec: 8 = [18.940,
16.320, 0.894, 6.144, 3.825, 2.908, 5.949, 2.000]
Key: 198: Value: wt: 1.0 distance: 2.626815730803073  vec: 8 = [15.380,
14.900, 0.871, 5.884, 3.268, 4.462, 5.795, 2.000]
Key: 79: Value: wt: 1.0 distance: 2.4487610767462544  vec: 8 = [16.160,
15.330, 0.864, 5.845, 3.395, 4.266, 5.795, 2.000]
Key: 198: Value: wt: 1.0 distance: 3.092561743802084  vec: 8 = [15.560,
14.890, 0.882, 5.776, 3.408, 4.972, 5.847, 2.000]
Key: 198: Value: wt: 1.0 distance: 1.9165859729642354  vec: 8 = [15.380,
14.660, 0.899, 5.477, 3.465, 3.600, 5.439, 2.000]
```

Canopy clustering

Let's check the canopy clustering command-line options. We will discuss the important and commonly-used parameters:

Parameters	Description
`--input (-i)`	Path to input directory
`--output (-o)`	Path to output directory
`--distanceMeasure (-dm)`	The class name given to the distance measure to be used
`--overwrite (-ow)`	Overwrite the input directory if it is present
`--clustering (-cl)`	If present, perform clustering after convergence of centroid
`--method (-xm)`	Sequential or MapReduce execution
`--t1 (-t1)`	T1 threshold value

Parameters	Description
`--t2 (-t2)`	T2 threshold value
`--t3 (-t3)`	T3 threshold value – reducer phase
`--t4 (-t4)`	T4 threshold value – r educer phase

We will use the same preprocessed sequence file as the input directory for canopy clustering:

```
mahout canopy -i clustering_seq -o clustering_canopy -dm org.apache.
mahout.common.distance.EuclideanDistanceMeasure -t1 1.0 -t2 2.0 -xm
mapreduce -c
```

The output directory has the following files, which can be displayed in the same manner as k-means:

```
hadoop fs -ls clustering_canopy

/user/ctiwary/clustering_canopy/clusteredPoints
/user/ctiwary/clustering_canopy/clusters-0-final
```

Fuzzy k-means

Let's check the fuzzy k-means clustering command-line options. We will discuss the important and commonly-used parameters:

Parameters	Description
`--input (-i)`	Path to input directory
`--output (-o)`	Path to output directory
`--output (-o)`	Path to output directory
`--distanceMeasure (-dm)`	The class name given to the distance measure to be used
`--clusters (-c)`	The input centroid as vectors in sequence format
`--numClusters (-k)`	The number of clusters to be generated
`--convergenceDelta (-cd)`	The convergence delta value
`--maxIter (-x)`	The maximum number of iterations to be performed
`--overwrite (-ow)`	Overwrite the input directory if present
`--clustering(-cl)`	If present, perform clustering after convergence of centroid
`--method (-xm)`	Sequential or MapReduce execution
`--m (-m)`	Coefficient normalization factor, must be greater than 1, controls the fuzziness of the clustering

We use the same processed sequence file as the input directory. Note that we pass an additional parameter -m as compared to the k-means, which is created by overlapping clusters:

```
mahout fkmeans -i clustering_seq -c kmeans_init_cluster -o
clustering_output_fkmeans -dm org.apache.mahout.common.distance.
EuclideanDistanceMeasure -x 10 -k 3 -ow --clustering -m 1.2
```

The output can be viewed using the ls utility of Hadoop:

```
hadoop fs -ls clustering_output_fkmeans
```

```
/user/ctiwary/clustering_output_fkmeans/_policy
/user/ctiwary/clustering_output_fkmeans/clusteredPoints
/user/ctiwary/clustering_output_fkmeans/clusters-0
/user/ctiwary/clustering_output_fkmeans/clusters-/user/ctiwary/
clustering_output_fkmeans/clusters-/user/ctiwary/clustering_output_
fkmeans/clusters-3-final
```

The last step is to see the clusters using clusterdump. The output is similar to what we discussed with k-means:

```
mahout clusterdump -i clustering_output_fkmeans/clusters-*-final
```

```
SV-4{n=66 c=[18.507, 16.207, 0.884, 6.176, 3.699, 3.584, 6.033, 1.951]
r=[1.251, 0.537, 0.015, 0.237, 0.163, 1.217, 0.244, 0.216]}
SV-200{n=72 c=[11.884, 13.244, 0.851, 5.224, 2.859, 4.749, 5.101, 2.907]
r=[0.744, 0.351, 0.022, 0.141, 0.150, 1.344, 0.178, 0.421]}
SV-16{n=70 c=[14.430, 14.352, 0.879, 5.526, 3.253, 2.730, 5.132, 1.113]
r=[1.063, 0.507, 0.017, 0.211, 0.161, 1.162, 0.287, 0.349]}
14/09/28 15:46:14 INFO clustering.ClusterDumper: Wrote 3 clusters
14/09/28 15:46:14 INFO driver.MahoutDriver: Program took 484 ms (Minutes:
0.008066666666666666)
```

Streaming k-means

Let's check the streaming k-means clustering command-line options, we will discuss the important and commonly-used parameters:

Parameters	Description
--input (-i)	Path to input directory
--output (-o)	Path to output directory
--output (-o)	Path to output directory

Parameters	Description
`--distanceMeasure (-dm)`	The class name given to the distance measure to be used
`--numClusters (-k)`	The k in k-means, denotes that approximately those many clusters will be created.
`--estimatedNumMapClusters (-km)`	The estimated number of clusters to use for the map phase of the job
`--maxIter (-x)`	The maximum number of iterations to be performed
`--overwrite (-ow)`	Overwrite the input directory if they are present
`--clustering (-cl)`	If present, perform clustering after convergence of the centroid
`--method (-xm)`	Sequential or MapReduce execution

We use the same processed sequence file as the input directory for the streaming of the k-means example:

```
mahout streamingkmeans -i clustering_seq -o clustering_output_
streamkmeans -sc org.apache.mahout.math.neighborhood.FastProjectionSearch
-dm org.apache.mahout.common.distance.EuclideanDistanceMeasure -k 3 -km 4
-ow


hadoop fs -ls clustering_output_streamkmeans


/user/ctiwary/clustering_output_streamkmeans/_SUCCESS
/user/ctiwary/clustering_output_streamkmeans/_logs
/user/ctiwary/clustering_output_streamkmeans/part-r-00000


hadoop fs -ls clustering_output_streamkmeans
Key: 0: Value: key = 1, weight = 61.00, vector = {0:18.725892857142846,2:
0.885567857142857,1:16.29571428571429,5:3.5416249999999985,7:1.9821428571
428572,6:6.062232142857143,3:6.208339285714282,4:3.7261250000000006}
Key: 1: Value: key = 2, weight = 74.00, vector = {0:14.594545454545454,2:
0.8789560606060605,1:14.435151515151516,5:2.6875030303030276,7:1.12121212
12121218,6:5.1750757575757556,3:5.550848484848486,4:3.2686818181818182}
Key: 2: Value: key = 0, weight = 75.00, vector = {0:11.844218749999998,2:
0.8507296875000001,1:13.221875000000006,5:4.575562499999999,7:2.906250000
0000004,6:5.0941406250000005,3:5.217984374999997,4:2.853718750000001}
```

A Mahout Java example

We will now discuss how to use the clustering algorithm discussed in Java code. Open the `MahoutClusteringExample.java` file from the `chapter7.src` package.

k-means

Define the distance measure to be used by the k-means clustering algorithm:

```
DistanceMeasure measure = new EuclideanDistanceMeasure();
```

We create the `Path` variable to the input sequence directory created in the preprocessing step:

```
Path inputSeq = newPath("clustering_seq")
```

The next step is to generate the random initial cluster seeds. We create the output directory path, where we save the initial cluster points. The path constructor with two arguments creates a folder with the name of the second argument inside the directory of the first argument. You could use a separate directory for the initial cluster directory too:

```
Path clusters = newPath(inputSeq, "random-seeds")
```

The `RandomSeedGenerator` class has the `buildRandom()` function for that. It takes as input the `Configuration` object, the input directory with the sequence files, the output directory in which the initial clusters are to be created, the number of clusters, and the distance measure.

The function returns the `Path` to the initial centroid directory:

```
clusters = RandomSeedGenerator.buildRandom(conf, inputSeqDir, clusters,
3,measure);
```

We then create the clustering output directory:

```
Path output = new Path("clustering_output");
```

We then invoke the `run` method of the `KmeansDriver` class, which runs the parallel implementation of the k-means clustering algorithm. The output will be in the same format as the one from the Mahout command-line example:

```
KMeansDriver.run(conf, inputSeqDir, clusters, output, 0.2,50, true, 0.0,
false);
```

We could estimate the number of clusters and initial cluster centroids using canopy clustering and then pass the same to KMeansDriver:

```
CanopyDriver.runJob(conf, inputSeqDir, output_canopy,measure,, (float)
3.1, (float) 2.1, true);
```

The initial clusters created by the preceding code line is passed to the runJob() method of the KmeansDriver class.

```
KMeansDriver.runJob(conf, inputSeqDir, output_canopy/clusters-0",
output,measure, "0.001", "10", true);
```

Note that we don't need to pass the number of clusters when we initialize the initial cluster centroids using canopy clustering.

Cluster evaluation

Mahout has some implementations for internal cluster evaluation. We will briefly discuss that.

The cluster evaluation requires passing a distance measure. We create the DistanceMeasure object as follows:

```
DistanceMeasure measure = new EuclideanDistanceMeasure();
We run the RepresentativePointsDriver run method which setsup the
ClusterEvaluator object properties.
RepresentativePointsDriver.run(conf, new Path("clustering_output_fkmeans/
clusters-3-final"),
new Path("clustering_output", "clusteredPoints"), new Path("clustering_
output_fkmeans"),
measure,
10, true);
```

We create the ClusterEvaluator object and pass the Configuration object and path to the cluster output directory:

```
ClusterEvaluator cv = new ClusterEvaluator(conf,new Path("clustering_
output/clusters-3-final"));
```

We invoke the respective functions to calculate the inter-cluster and intra cluster density of the clusters:

```
System.out.println(cv.interClusterDensity());
System.out.println(cv.intraClusterDensity());
```

We can calculate the evaluation metrics for other clustering algorithms too.

Summary

In this chapter, we discussed different clustering algorithms in Mahout. We discussed the concept of k-means to better understand the clustering process, looked at command-line examples of various clustering algorithms, and finally discussed implementing k-means using Mahout Java API. I would encourage you to experiment with the different datasets and different settings/configurations of each algorithm to get a deeper understanding of the usage of clustering algorithms.

In the next chapter, we are going to discuss Mahout on top of Apache Spark. Mahout is being ported to Spark in Mahout 1.0, so carefully read this next chapter. It will help you get started with Mahout 1.0 when it is released.

8
New Paradigm in Mahout

Mahout started out primarily as a Java MapReduce package to run distributed and scalable machine learning algorithms on top of Hadoop. As the Mahout Project matures, it has taken a decision to move out of MapReduce and embrace Apache Spark and other distributed processing frameworks, such as H20, with a focus on *write once and run on multiple platforms*. In this chapter, we are going to discuss:

- Limitations of MapReduce
- Apache Spark
- In-core binding
- Out-of-core binding

MapReduce and HDFS were two paradigms largely responsible for a quantum shift in data processing capability. With increased capabilities, we learned to imagine larger problems that kick started a whole new industry of Big Data Analytics. The last decade has been amazing for solving data-related problems. However, in recent times, a lot of effort has been put into developing processing paradigms beyond MapReduce. These efforts are either aimed at replacing MapReduce or augmenting the processing framework. The examples are Impala, Drill, Spark, and so on.

Moving beyond MapReduce

Let's discuss why we need to move beyond MapReduce. Based on the scenario and use case, there are many advantages and limitations of MapReduce. In this section, we will concern ourselves with the limitations that impact machine learning use cases.

Firstly, MapReduce is not feasible when the intermediate processes need to talk to each other. A lot of machine learning algorithms need to work based on a shared global state, which is difficult to implement with MapReduce.

Secondly, quite a few problems are difficult to break down into map and reduce phases. Mahout is porting to Apache Spark, which works on top of HDFS and provides a processing paradigm other than MapReduce.

Apache Spark

Spark was developed as a general-purpose engine for large-scale data processing. It recently released its 1.0 version. Spark has two important features.

The first feature that Spark has is a **resilient distributed dataset (RDD)**. This is a collection of elements partitioned across the nodes of a cluster, which can be operated on in parallel. A file on HDFS or any existing Scala collection can be converted to an RDD collection, and any operation on it can be executed in parallel. RDDs can also be requested to persist in memory, which leads to efficient parallel operations. RDDs have automatic fail-over support and can recover from node failures.

The second important feature of Spark is the concept of shared variables and is used primarily during parallel operations. Spark has support for two types of shared variables: *broadcast variables* and *accumulators*. Broadcast variables are used as a cache, it stores the value of the variable in memory on all the nodes, accumulators are variables that can only be added up and is used in scenarios like counters, sums, and so on. The shared variables are available across all nodes for a parallel job.

Configuring Spark with Mahout

Download Spark somewhere in your home drive using the following command:

```
wget http://d3kbcqa49mib13.cloudfront.net/spark-0.9.1.tgz
```

Make sure you get the same version of Spark with which the current development version of Mahout was compiled. The trunk I checked out was compiled using Spark 0.9.1. This is required, as this feature is not yet released, and Mahout trunk and Spark versions will keep changing till it is released. To check for the latest versions of Spark and Mahout trunk, please visit `https://github.com/apache/mahout`.

Copy the downloaded folder to `/usr/local` and unpack using `tar`. After unpacking, change to the `spark` directory where you unpacked and type the following command to build it:

```
sbt/sbt assembly
```

Check out the latest Mahout trunk using **subversion** (**svn**). svn is an open source version control system. It helps you keep track of a collection of files and folders:

```
svn co https://svn.apache.org/repos/asf/mahout/trunk/ mahout-spark
```

Run the following commands:

```
cd mahout-spark
mvn clean
mvn compile
mvn install
```

The next step is to go back to the Spark directory and type the following command to start Spark:

```
sbin/start-all.sh
```

After Spark has started, open the URL http://localhost:8080 to check the Spark cluster details.

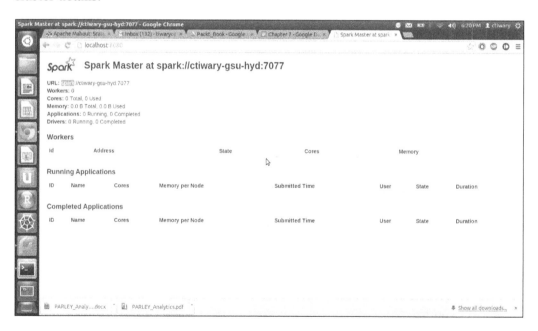

Copy the URL field from the webpage. To stop Spark later on, we can use the following command:

```
sbin/stop-all.sh
```

Move back to the Mahout directory. We need to export the following variables for the Mahout shell to work:

```
export MAHOUT_HOME=[ Path to Mahout Directory]
export SPARK_HOME=[Path to the Spark Directory]
export MASTER=[url of the Spark master]
```

In my case, the values for the environment variables are:

```
export MAHOUT_HOME=<your path here>/mahout-spark
export SPARK_HOME=<your path here>/spark
export MASTER=spark://<your username>:7077
```

If you are following the instructions as per the book, then the natural place would be usr/local.

After the variables have been exported, we will start the Mahout shell:

```
bin/mahout spark-shell
```

To exit from the shell, we can type the following command on Mahout shell:

```
exit()
```

Basics of Mahout Scala DSL

Mahout and Spark are being developed to abstract away the details of programming a distributed system. We don't have to worry about the intricacies of parallel programming, and we can concentrate on solving the machine learning task at hand.

Mahout Scala and Spark Bindings are aimed at providing an R-like feel to the Mahout shell. If you are familiar with R, you will be aware of its ease while working with linear algebra. One can basically type in the formula and see the execution. Right now, Mahout and Spark binding supports three major types: **distributed row matrices (DRM)**, in-core vectors, and in-core matrices.

Let's start with practicing some command-line examples. Remember to go back to the Spark directory and run the start-all.sh script. Then, go back to the Mahout directory, export all the required environment variables, and run the command to get the shell.

Imports

The following two Scala imports are typically used to enable Mahout Scala DSL bindings for linear algebra. We can type them directly to the command line:

```
import org.apache.mahout.math._
import scalabindings._
//To use R like dialect use
import RlikeOps._
```

Another option is to use the matlab-like dialect by typing:

```
import MatlabLikeOps._
```

In this chapter, we are going to restrict ourselves to the R-like dialect.

In-core types

Vector and Matrices are of type in-core or in-memory. We will try out some basic commands to get a feel of the linear algebra operations possible.

Vector

We will first discuss vectors and then cover matrices. We will see some examples of operations that can be performed on vectors.

Initializing a vector inline

Dense vector: The dense vector is a vector with relatively fewer zero elements. On the Mahout command line, please type the following command to initialize a dense vector:

```
mahout>val denseVec1: Vector = (1.0, 1.1, 1.2)
```

Each element is prefixed by its index, which starts with 0. The output of the command executed is given as follows:

```
denseVec1: org.apache.mahout.math.Vector = {0:1.0,1:1.1,2:1.2}
```

Sparse vector: Sparse vector is a vector with a relatively large number of zero elements. On the Mahout command line, please type the following command to initialize a sparse vector:

```
mahout>val sparseVec = svec((5 -> 1) :: (10 -> 2.0) :: Nil)
```

The output of the command executed is given in the following command line. As we can see it creates `RandomAcessSparseVector`:

```
sparseVec:org.apache.mahout.math.RandomAccessSparseVector =
{10:2.0,5:1.0}
```

Accessing elements of a vector

Vectors are accessed using the index number. For example, to access the third element, we will use the index 2 as the index starts with zero. Type the following command on the Mahout command line:

```
mahout>denseVec1(2)
```

The result is the value of element 3 with the corresponding data type:

```
res13: Double = 1.2
```

Setting values of an element

Again, we can use the index to set the value of a particular element of a vector. Let's set the third element to the value 2:

```
mahout> denseVec1(2)=2
mahout> denseVec1
res18: org.apache.mahout.math.Vector = {0:1.0,1:1.1,2:2.0}
```

Vector arithmetic

In this section, we will discuss some common vector arithmetic operations such as addition, division, and multiplication. For example, let's create a new dense vector with the `denseVec2` name. Input the following command on the Mahout command line, which will initialize the vector:

```
mahout> val denseVec2: Vector = (1.0, 1.1, 5.5)
```

The result is the following dense vector:

```
denseVec2: org.apache.mahout.math.Vector = {0:1.0,1:1.1,2:5.5}
```

This is the multiplication of two vectors:

```
mahout> val multilpy_vec=denseVec1*denseVec2
multilpy_vec: org.apache.mahout.math.Vector = {0:1.0,1:1.2100000000000002
,2:6.6}
```

This is the division of two vectors:

```
mahout> val divide_vec=denseVec1/denseVec2
divide_vec: org.apache.mahout.math.Vector = {0:1.0,1:1.0,2:0.218181818181
81817}
```

This is the addition of two vectors:

```
mahout> val add_vec=denseVec1+denseVec2
add_vec: org.apache.mahout.math.Vector = {0:2.0,1:2.2,2:6.7}
```

This is the subtraction of two vectors:

```
mahout> val sub_vec=denseVec1-denseVec2
sub_vec: org.apache.mahout.math.Vector = {2:-4.3}
```

Vector operations with a scalar

In the previous section, we discussed arithmetic operations on a vector. Now, we will see the results of scalar operations on a vector.

The result of adding a scalar to a vector is that all elements are incremented by the value of the scalar. For example, the following command adds five to all the elements of the vector:

```
mahout> val add_scalr=denseVec1+5
add_scalr: org.apache.mahout.math.Vector = {0:6.0,1:6.1,2:6.2}
```

Similar to the preceding command, this operation subtracts five from each of the element in the vector:

```
mahout> val sub_scalr=denseVec1-5
sub_scalr: org.apache.mahout.math.Vector = {0:-4.0,1:-3.9,2:-3.8}
```

The following scalar operation multiplies all the elements by five:

```
mahout> val mul_scalr=denseVec1*5
mul_scalr: org.apache.mahout.math.Vector = {0:5.0,1:5.5,2:6.0}
```

Lastly, division by a scalar divides all the elements by five:

```
mahout> val div_scalr=denseVec1/5
div_scalr: org.apache.mahout.math.Vector = {0:0.2,1:0.22000000000000003,2
:0.24}
```

Matrix

We will now have a look at a matrix and the operations that can be performed on it.

Initializing the matrix

The inline initialization of a matrix, either dense or sparse, is always performed row-wise.

- Dense matrix:

```
mahout> val A = dense((1, 2, 3), (3, 4, 5))
A: org.apache.mahout.math.DenseMatrix =
{
  0   =>..{0:1.0,1:2.0,2:3.0}
  1   =>..{0:3.0,1:4.0,2:5.0}
}
```

- Sparse matrix:

```
val A = sparse(
(1, 3) :: Nil,
(0, 2) :: (1, 2.5) :: Nil
)
```

- Diagonal matrix:

```
mahout> val x=diag(10, 3)
x: org.apache.mahout.math.DiagonalMatrix =
{
  0   =>..{0:10.0}
  1   =>..{1:10.0}
  2   =>..{2:10.0}
}
```

- Identity matrix:

```
mahout> val x = eye(5)
x: org.apache.mahout.math.DiagonalMatrix =
{
  0   =>..{0:1.0}
  1   =>..{1:1.0}
  2   =>..{2:1.0}
  3   =>..{3:1.0}
  4   =>..{4:1.0}
}
```

Accessing elements of a matrix

We will create a matrix called `matrix_example`, and then slice and dice it:

```
mahout> val matrix_example = dense((1, 2, 3), (3, 4, 5))
matrix_example: org.apache.mahout.math.DenseMatrix =
{
  0   =>   {0:1.0,1:2.0,2:3.0}
  1   =>   {0:3.0,1:4.0,2:5.0}
}
```

Accessing the second element of the second row:

```
mahout> matrix_example(1,1)
res35: Double = 4.0
```

Accessing the first element of the first row:

```
mahout> matrix_example(0,0)
res36: Double = 1.0
```

Fetching a complete row, in this case the second row:

```
mahout> val rowVec=matrix_example(1,::)
rowVec: org.apache.mahout.math.Vector = {0:3.0,1:4.0,2:5.0}
```

Fetching a complete row, in this case the first row:

```
mahout> val rowVec=matrix_example(0,::)
rowVec: org.apache.mahout.math.Vector = {0:1.0,1:2.0,2:3.0}
```

Fetching a complete column, in this case the first column:

```
mahout> val rowVec=matrix_example(::,0)
rowVec: org.apache.mahout.math.Vector = {0:1.0,1:3.0}
```

Fetching the second column:

```
mahout> val rowVec=matrix_example(::,1)
rowVec: org.apache.mahout.math.Vector = {0:2.0,1:4.0}
```

Setting the matrix row, in this case the first row:

```
mahout> matrix_example(1,::)=(10,9,6)
res45: org.apache.mahout.math.Vector = {0:10.0,1:9.0,2:6.0}
mahout> matrix_example
res46: org.apache.mahout.math.DenseMatrix =
```

```
{
  0  =>  {0:1.0,1:9.0,2:3.0}
  1  =>  {0:10.0,1:9.0,2:6.0}
}
```

Fetching the sub-slices of a row, row 1 first two elements:

```
mahout> matrix_example(0,0 to 1)=(44,55)
res49: org.apache.mahout.math.Vector = {0:44.0,1:55.0}
```

Fetching the sub-slices of a row, row 2 second and third elements:

```
mahout> matrix_example(1,1 to 2)=(44,55)
res50: org.apache.mahout.math.Vector = {0:44.0,1:55.0}
```

Setting the matrix column

We will discuss the column operations on a matrix. Let's see how to set the value of an entire column of a matrix. Let's set the values of column 2. As indexing starts from 0, we access column 2 by index:

```
mahout> matrix_example(::,1)=(9,6)
res43: org.apache.mahout.math.Vector = {0:9.0,1:6.0}
```

To fetch the number of rows of a matrix, we need to access the nrow property:

```
mahout> matrix_example.nrow
res52: Int = 2
```

Similarly, to fetch the number of columns of a matrix, we access the ncol property:

```
mahout> matrix_example.ncol
res57: Int = 3
```

To fetch the sum of all columns, we use colSums:

```
mahout> matrix_example.colSums
res58: org.apache.mahout.math.Vector = {0:54.0,1:99.0,2:58.0}
```

Lastly, to fetch the sum of rows, we use rowSums:

```
mahout> matrix_example.rowSums
res59: org.apache.mahout.math.Vector = {0:102.0,1:109.0}
```

Copy by reference

Matrices are assigned by reference and not as a copy, hence we need to take care of the pitfalls associated with it. Here's an example of the same:

```
mahout> val ex1 = matrix_example
ex1: org.apache.mahout.math.DenseMatrix =
{
  0   =>..{0:1.0,1:2.0,2:3.0}
  1   =>..{0:3.0,1:4.0,2:5.0}
}
mahout> ex1 +=5.0
res5: org.apache.mahout.math.Matrix =
{
  0   =>..{0:6.0,1:7.0,2:8.0}
  1   =>..{0:8.0,1:9.0,2:10.0}
}
mahout> ex1
res6: org.apache.mahout.math.DenseMatrix =
{
  0   =>..{0:6.0,1:7.0,2:8.0}
  1   =>..{0:8.0,1:9.0,2:10.0}
}
mahout> matrix_example
res7: org.apache.mahout.math.DenseMatrix =
{
  0   =>..{0:6.0,1:7.0,2:8.0}
  1   =>..{0:8.0,1:9.0,2:10.0}
}
```

We saw that the original matrix_example matrix also got modified when we modified the matrix ex1, which was a copy of the original matrix `matrix_example`. To address this behavior, we can use clones. To keep the previous matrix value intact, we can use the `clone` command:

```
mahout> val ex1 = matrix_example clone
warning: there were 1 feature warning(s); re-run with -feature for
details
ex1: org.apache.mahout.math.Matrix =
{
  0   =>   {0:6.0,1:7.0,2:8.0}
  1   =>   {0:8.0,1:9.0,2:10.0}
}
mahout> ex1 +=5.0
res8: org.apache.mahout.math.Matrix =
{
```

```
  0  =>  {0:11.0,1:12.0,2:13.0}
  1  =>  {0:13.0,1:14.0,2:15.0}
}
mahout> matrix_example
res9: org.apache.mahout.math.DenseMatrix =
{
  0  =>  {0:6.0,1:7.0,2:8.0}
  1  =>  {0:8.0,1:9.0,2:10.0}
}
```

Spark Mahout basics

We will now focus on Mahout Spark's DRM. DRM, once loaded into Spark, is partitioned by rows of the DRM.

Initializing the Spark context

Many operations on the DRM will require a Spark context. To initialize Mahout with the Spark session, we create the implicit variable `mahoutCtx` as the Spark context:

```
implicit val mahoutCtx = mahoutSparkContext(
masterUrl = "spark://ctiwary-gsu-hyd:7077",
appName = "MahoutLocalContext"
)
We will import some import
// Import matrix, vector types, etc.
import org.apache.mahout.math._
// Import scala bindings operations
import scalabindings._
// Enable R-like dialect in scala bindings
import RLikeOps._
// Import distributed matrix apis
import drm._
// Import R-like distributed dialect
import RLikeDrmOps._
// Those are needed for Spark-specific
// operations such as context creation.
// 100% engine-agnostic code does not
// require these.
import org.apache.mahout.sparkbindings._
// A good idea when working with mixed
// scala/java iterators and collections
import collection._
import JavaConversions._
```

The `MahoutLocalContext` application UI can be accessed on `http://localhost:4041/`.

Now, we need to create an in-core matrix with the `in_core_matrix` name and a distributed matrix called `parallel_matrix`. The following command will initialize the respective matrices:

```
val in_core_matrix = dense((1, 2, 3), (3, 4, 5))
val parallel_matrix = drmParallelize(in_core_matrix)

mahout> val parallel_matrix = drmParallelize(in_core_matrix)
parallel_matrix: org.apache.mahout.math.drm.CheckpointedDrm[Int] = org.
apache.mahout.sparkbindings.drm.CheckpointedDrmSpark@2f43cbcc


parallel_matrix.writeDRM(path="testSparkWrite")

check hadoop fs -ls testSparkWrite

val testRead = drmFromHDFS(path = "testSparkWrite")
```

Mahout Spark binding has two types of actions, optimizer actions and computational actions.

Optimizer actions

Optimizer actions, when performed on a DRM operation, don't trigger the actual computation but they materialize the physical plan of execution. Optimizer actions are backed by `CheckpointedDRM`, which acts as a cutoff boundary for the optimizer actions. Optimizer actions can be triggered explicitly by `DRMLike#checkpoint()`.

Let's try to understand with the help of the following two examples:

```
val A = drmParallelize (...)
val B = drmParallelize (...)
val C = A %*% B.t
val D = C.t
val E = C.t %*% C
D.writeDRM(..path..)
E.writeDRM(..path..)
```

In this example, the optimizer optimizes two pipelines separately, the one calculating D and the other calculating E using the same matrices A and B as root of both computations. Now, let's consider the following modified example:

```
val A = drmParallelize (...)
val B = drmParallelize (...)
val C = (A %*% B.t).checkpoint
val D = C.t
val E = C.t %*% C
D.writeDRM(..path..)
E.writeDRM(..path..)
```

In this example (which is functionally equivalent to the previous one), the optimizer considers three separate pipelines of execution: C, D, and E while caching the optimized plan and intermediate result for C into the Spark cache. Introducing checkpoints may improve *wall time* since matrices D and E will be triggered for action.

In both of the examples, nothing happens in the backend until a computational action is triggered for either of E or D.

It doesn't matter how many times `checkpointing` is called on a logical operator, the same logical operator will be optimized and set for caching policy only once.

Computational actions

Computational actions lead to results being computed and optionally placed into the Spark cache. Such actions will also lazily and implicitly trigger linalg optimizer checkpointing. Currently, computational actions include `writeDrm()`, `collect()`, `blockify()`. They can sometimes also be triggered implicitly by an optimizer activity beyond the current checkpoint's cutoff (if checkpointed but not computed and cached yet) to run some cost estimates necessary for the optimizer beyond checkpointing, potentially future actions associated with DRM sub-blocking.

For instance, in the second example, running `E.writeDrm(path)` will trigger computational actions for E and, implicitly, for C.

All these rules follow the same patterns as for the in-core arguments.

Caching in Spark's block manager

Every checkpoint can be, and by default, is, pushed into Spark's memory block manager. The default policy is MEMORY_ONLY, but the storage level can be specified explicitly as a parameter to the checkpoint() call. The actual push of data to the memory block manager happens no sooner than an actual partition computation occurs for the first time (that is, at the first occurrence of a computational action of the pipeline involving the result in question). Five Checkpointed DRMs may later be explicitly uncached from block manager (asynchronously) if desired, for example:

```
val drmA = (/*..drm expression..*/).checkpoint(CacheHint.MEMORY_AND_DISK)
... some computational actions involving drmA
... drmA is not needed anymore
drmA.uncache()
```

If the argument is not cached by the time the uncache() call has occurred, nothing of substance happens.

Linear regression with Mahout Spark

We will discuss the linear regression example mentioned on the Mahout Wiki. Let's first create the training data in the form of a parallel DRM:

```
val drmData = drmParallelize(dense(
  (2, 2, 10.5, 10, 29.509541),   // Apple Cinnamon Cheerios
  (1, 2, 12,   12, 18.042851),   // Cap'n'Crunch
  (1, 1, 12,   13, 22.736446),   // Cocoa Puffs
  (2, 1, 11,   13, 32.207582),   // Froot Loops
  (1, 2, 12,   11, 21.871292),   // Honey Graham Ohs
  (2, 1, 16,   8,  36.187559),   // Wheaties Honey Gold
  (6, 2, 17,   1,  50.764999),   // Cheerios
  (3, 2, 13,   7,  40.400208),   // Clusters
  (3, 3, 13,   4,  45.811716)),  // Great Grains Pecan
  numPartitions = 2);
```

The first four columns will be our feature vector and the last column will be our target variable. We will separate out the feature matrix and the target vector, drmX being the feature matrix and y being the target vector:

```
val drmX = drmData(::, 0 until 4)
```

The target variable is collected into the memory using the collect method:

```
val y = drmData.collect(::, 4)
```

The next step is to introduce the bias column to the feature matrix; we will define a `Scala` function to do the same:

```scala
val drmXwithBiasColumn = drmX.mapBlock(ncol = drmX.ncol + 1) {
  case(keys, block) =>
    // create a new block with an additional column
    val blockWithBiasColumn = block.like(block.nrow, block.ncol + 1)
    // copy data from current block into the new block
    blockWithBiasColumn(::, 0 until block.ncol) := block
    // last column consists of ones
    blockWithBiasColumn(::, block.ncol) := 1

    keys -> blockWithBiasColumn
}
```

Now, to estimate the value of parameter vector β, we will use the approach of **ordinary least square (OLS)**. OLS minimizes the sum of residual squares between the actual target value and the predicted value. We have a closed-form expression for estimating β as $\left(X^T X \right)^{-1} X^T Y$.

We compute $\left(X^T X \right)$ first using the following statement:

```scala
val drmXtX = (drmX.t %*% drmX).collect
```

The `.t()` function returns the transpose and `%*%` is the multiplication symbol.

Similarly, we compute $X^T Y$:

```scala
val drmXty = (drmX.t %*% y).collect(::, 0)
```

Then, we call the `solve()` function to return the value of β. We represent the same in the form of a function:

```scala
def ols(drmX: DrmLike[Int], y: Vector) = {
  val XtX = (drmX.t %*% drmX).collect
  val Xty = (drmX.t %*% y).collect(::, 0)
  solve(XtX, Xty)
}
```

To determine the goodness of fit, we will use the following function:

```scala
def goodnessOfFit(drmX: DrmLike[Int], beta: Vector, y: Vector) = {
  val fittedY = (drmX %*% beta).collect(::, 0)
  (y - fittedY).norm(2)
}
```

We will call the function using the following commands:

```
val betaWithBiasTerm = ols(drmXwithBiasColumn, y)
goodnessOfFit(drmXwithBiasColumn, betaWithBiasTerm, y)
```

Summary

We briefly discussed Mahout and Spark bindings. This is the future of Mahout, though a production-ready release is some time away. We learned the basic operations that can be performed on the various data structures and went through an example of applying these techniques to build a machine learning algorithm. I would encourage you to keep yourself updated on the development of Mahout and Spark bindings, and the best way would be to follow the Mahout Wiki.

In the next chapter, we will discuss end-to-end practical use cases of customer analytics. Most of the techniques used so far will be put into practice, and you will get an idea of a real-life analytics project.

Case Study – Churn Analytics and Customer Segmentation

In this chapter, we are going to discuss the steps involved in a machine learning project from start to finish. We will cover all the important steps that need to be performed for a successful machine learning project. We will use a couple of examples from customer analytics to walk through the process. The topics covered in this chapter are:

- Churn analytics
- Customer segmentation

Churn analytics

Until now, in this book, we have discussed multiple important machine learning concepts and algorithms and their implementation/usage in Mahout. We also saw multiple examples of using machine learning algorithms with Mahout. We are now going to focus on end-to-end case studies, keeping a specific business problem in mind. This chapter and the next will help you put the pieces together and get an overview of a complete analytics project. We will first look at churn prediction.

The goal of churn analytics is to understand the primary drivers to churn and predict churn. Churn can have a very specific meaning depending upon the industry or even the organization we are talking about, but in general it is related to the extension of the contract between a service provider and a subscriber. The contract is valid until the service term period, and then is up for renewal at the end of the contract term period. For example, postpaid telecom subscribers renew their contract with the telecom provider every month. If they choose to, they can end the relationship any month by terminating the contract at the end of that month.

In this case, the subscription term is monthly and the termination of the contract will be considered as churning. It is of paramount importance for a telecom provider to be able to identify a subscriber at risk of churning so that they can be retained. Retention could be in terms of outbound calls to solve any issues the subscriber is facing, an offer or discount, a special plan, and so on. But to do any of this, we need to know whether the subscriber is going to churn and that too a few months in advance so that the retention process has enough time. So, there are two components to a churn model, a prediction about a subscriber churning and, the time period within which the subscriber will churn.

To predict churn, say n month before it happens, we need to build the model on signals that it is n month before the churn date. Typically, most recent n months of data have to be ignored from the churn date for the churned account and n months, from the maximum date for active accounts. For example, let's check the following data. Let's assume that the maximum date until which data is to be considered is 2014-12-31 and the minimum date is 2012-01-01. We have a total of three years of historical data. We will discuss the account inclusion criteria for churn analytics based upon sample data in the following table:

Account	Status	Signup date	Churn date
A	Churned	2014-06-30	2014-11-30
B	Churned	2013-01-01	2014-08-31
C	Churned	2012-02-20	

Account A and B are churned and C is active. Also let's assume that the data under consideration is six months. We are going to only include accounts with six months' worth of data. Prediction needs to be made three months in advance. We will ignore three months of data from the churn date for churned accounts and three months of data from the maximum date for active accounts.

For account A, data needs to be considered from 2014-11-90 - 90 days = 2014-09-01 and for account B 2014-08-31 - 90 days = 2014-06-02. Similarly, for active account C we subtract 90 days from the maximum date, 2014-12-31 - 90 days = 2014-10-02. Now the next step is to ensure that all accounts have at least six months of data after ignoring three months. To calculate this, we need to subtract the considered date, for example 2014-09-01 for Account A from either the signup date or the earliest usage date, whichever is the most recent. In our sample data, all the signup dates are more recent than the minimum date, so we will use the signup date column. We calculate the number of days of usable data by subtracting the cut-off date from the signup date as follows:

- A → 2014-09-01 - 2014-06-30 = 64 days

- B → 2014-06-02 - 2013-01-01 = 518 days
- C → 2014-10-02 - 2012-02-02 = 974 days

We have to drop account A as it only has 64 days of usable data and we need a minimum of 180 days of data. For accounts B and C, we are going to use six months of data. Data to be considered is as follows:

- A → 2014-06-02 – 180 days = 2013-12-04, between 2014-06-02 and 2013-12-04
- B → 2014-10-02 – 180 days = 2014-04-05, between 2014-10-02 and 2014-04-05

Now we have decided which accounts are to be included and the time period within which the data has to be considered for each account. Feature engineering needs to be done on this selected dataset. An account inclusion criteria and time period for data to be considered is very important for churn analytics and should be done carefully.

Survival analysis is another popular approach for modeling churn but we will not go into that much.

Getting the data

To start with our case study, we first need to get the data. We will look at a dataset that contains information about the subscriber from the telecom domain and their status information.

The data can be downloaded from `http://www.sgi.com/tech/mlc/db/` or found in the code base directory that comes with the book. We need to download the `churn.all`, `churn.data`, `churn.names`, and `churn.test` files. The `churn.all` file has 5000 rows and 21 columns. The `churn.data` and `churn.test` files are different samples from the same `churn.all` file and could be used for training and testing the model. The `churn.names` file has the names of all the columns in the data files. Let's see the preprocessing step for the downloaded file `churn.data`; the file `churn.all` present in the directory `learningApacheMahout/data/chapter9` is already preprocessed.

The first step is to remove the white spaces from the file. To do this, we use the `sed` command, which takes `\s`, representing white spaces, as the search pattern and a blank as the replacement:

```
sed -i 's/\s//g' churn.all
```

The second step is to replace `False.` with `False` and `True.` with `True`:

```
sed -i 's/False./False/g' churn.all
sed -i 's/True./True/g' churn.all
```

Finally, we add the header line. The `sed` command matches the start of the first line and replaces it with the header information:

```
sed -i '1s/^/state,account length,area code,phone number,international
plan,voice mail plan,number vmail messages,total day minutes,total
day calls,total day charge,total eve minutes,total eve calls,total eve
charge,total night minutes,total night calls,total night charge,total
intl minutes,total intl calls,total intl charge,number customer service
calls,Status\n/' churn.all
```

In this dataset, the target variable is the last column, *Status,* which stores the information about whether a user churned or not. *True* stands for churn customers and *False* for active. We have a total of 4293 active and 707 churn customers in the dataset.

Let's have a look at the column definition; this is a good starting point to understand a dataset:

Column	Data Type
State	Discrete
account length	Continuous
area code	Continuous
phone number	Discrete
international plan	Discrete
voice mail plan	Discrete
number v-mail messages	Continuous
total day minutes	Continuous
total day calls	Continuous
total day charge	Continuous
total eve minutes	Continuous
total eve calls	Continuous
total eve charge	Continuous
total night minutes	Continuous
total night calls	Continuous
total night charge	Continuous
total intl minutes	Continuous
total intl calls	Continuous
total intl charge	Continuous
number customer service calls	Continuous
Status	Discrete

The dataset, as seen in this table, has various telecom service usage metrics from rows eight to 19. They cover attributes such as total number of calls, total charge, and total minutes used by different slices of the data. The slices include time, day or night, and usage type such as international call. Row 20 has the number of customer service calls made and row 21 is the status of the subscriber, which is our target variable.

This dataset doesn't provide any scope for account exclusion or selecting the time period, as the information is not available. We assume that data for all the subscribers has been collected for the same time duration; being in the same time period is desirable but not necessary. What is meant is that for all subscribers the data is collected for the same n months irrespective of the time period. Having data collected over the same duration leads to an apple-to-apple comparison. This is a compulsory precondition, as without this it would be difficult to combine all the subscribers into one feature set.

Data exploration

Data exploration is a very important part of any analytics project and quite a bit of effort goes into it. Primarily, the objective of exploration is to get a good idea about how the data looks, preprocess data to remove outliers, and get cues towards feature engineering. We are going to use R for our data exploration. The other tools that can be used are SAS, Excel, Python, and so on.

Installing R

Open the file /etc/apt/sources.list in a text editor and add the following line of code to the file. For a different Ubuntu version, the final argument would be different depending on the OS version:

```
deb http://cran.rstudio.com/bin/linux/ubuntu precise/
```

To install the complete R system, type the following command on the terminal:

```
sudo apt-get update
sudo apt-get install r-base
```

Type R on the terminal, which will start the R prompt.

To read the csv into a data frame, please execute the following command on the R prompt:

```
churn_data<-read.csv("churn.all",header=T)
```

The `read.csv` method takes the file name as the first argument. The second argument, set as `True`, treats the first line as the header line.

Type the following command to view the data frame created:

```
View(churn_data)
```

Summary statistics

As a first step, we will look at the summary statistics of the data. The summary statistics include looking at the min, max, median, median, the 1st and 3rd quartile of continuous variables, and the frequency count of categorical variables. It gives us a summarized understanding of the data, its centrality, and spread. We will contrast the overall summary statistics with the summary of only churn and only active subscribers.

To get the summary of all the data, type the following command:

```
summary_all<-summary(churn_data)
```

To get the summary of all churned customers, we call the `summary` function with, data of all churned customers. The `subset` function filters data based on the condition `Status==True`:

```
summary_churn<-summary(subset(churn_data,Status=='TRUE'))
```

To get the summary of all active customers, we call the `summary` function with data of all active customers. The `subset` function filters data based upon the condition `Status=='False'`:

```
summary_active<-summary(subset(churn_data,Status=='FALSE'))
```

To combine all the data frames into one file, we call the function `rbind()` on the three data frames and write to a `csv` file:

```
write.csv(rbind(summary_all,summary_churn,summary_active),file="summary_
file.csv")
```

The pattern to observe while looking at the `summary` file is to observe substantial difference between the summaries of churn and active customers, especially the mean, median, and the 1st and 3rd quartile. For example, let's look at the summary statistics of the feature *Total day calls* in the following table. The feature doesn't seem to have any distinguishing difference on its own:

Total day calls		
All subscribers	Churn subscribers	Active subscribers
1st Qu.: 87	1st Qu.: 88.0	1st Qu.: 87.0

Median :100	Median :101.0	Median: 100.0
Mean: 100	Mean: 100.8	Mean: 99.9
3rd Qu.:113	3rd Qu.:115.0	3rd Qu.:113.0

On the other hand, the feature *number of v-mail messages* does have distinguishing summary statistics. We can see that the churn customer has significantly lower v-mail messages. Now, that could be because of a lower number of v-mail subscriptions for the churn customer. We can see the summary statistics of v-mail messages in the following table:

Number of v-mail messages		
All subscribers	**Churn subscribers**	**Active subscribers**
1st Qu.: 0.000	1st Qu.: 0.000	1st Qu.: 0.000
Median: 0.000	Median: 0.000	Median: 0.000
Mean: 7.755	Mean: 4.496	Mean: 8.292
3rd Qu.: 17.000	3rd Qu.: 0.000	3rd Qu.: 20.000

Exploring the datasets helps us to understand patterns and validate the results after modelling.

Correlation

It is a good practice to remove the strongly correlated variables from the feature set; both strong positively and strong negatively correlated features need to be removed. We will check the correlation between numerical variables. Using R, we will first remove the non-numeric variables:

```
cor_data<-churn_data
cor_data$Status<-NULL
cor_data$voice.mail.plan<-NULL
cor_data$international.plan <-NULL
cor_data$phone.number<-NULL
cor_data$state<-NULL
```

We will then calculate the correlation, which returns a correlation matrix:

```
correlation_all<-cor(cor_data)
write.csv(correlation_all,file="correlation_file.csv")
```

Looking at `correlation_file.csv`, we can see that four pairs of columns are heavily correlated and we should remove them:

```
churn_data$total.day.charge<-NULL
churn_data$total.eve.charge<-NULL
churn_data$total.night.charge<-NULL
churn_data$total.intl.charge<-NULL
```

We will remove the features *phone number* and *state*.

```
churn_data$state<-NULL
churn_data$phone.number<-NULL
write.csv(churn_data,file="churn_data_clean.all.csv",row.names = F)
```

We need to remove these columns from all the files.

Another way of removing correlation is to perform dimensionality reduction such as PCA. This is the preferred approach if the dimensionality of the dataset is very high.

Feature engineering

Looking at the dataset, the scope of feature engineering looks a bit limited. The dimensionality is low and we don't have missing values. There is some scope for manual feature construction though, and we can use that to introduce some domain knowledge. The numeric features that we have measure how many calls a user makes, the frequency of the usage and the total time spent talking, the volume of the usage. The features like *total day calls* and *total eve calls* measure frequency of usage whereas features such as *total day minutes* and *total eve minutes* measure volume of usage. Another interesting feature to look at would be the average minutes per call. We can measure the average by dividing the *total minutes* by *total calls*, for example, the feature *average minutes per day call = total day minutes / total day calls* and similarly, *average minutes per eve call = total eve minutes/ total eve calls*.

> Always spend some time figuring out ways to enrich the feature representation by using the manual feature construction. This step is mostly guided by data exploration and domain knowledge. If you don't have knowledge about a particular domain, reading about it and talking to business users will definitely lead to additional insights.

To calculate the average in R, we need to execute the following commands:

```
churn_data$avg.minute.day<-churn_data$total.day.minutes/churn_data$total.day.calls

churn_data$avg.minute.eve<-churn_data$total.eve.minutes/churn_data$total.eve.calls
```

```
churn_data$avg.minute.night<-churn_data$total.night.minutes/churn_
data$total.night.calls

churn_data$avg.minute.intl<-churn_data$total.intl.minutes/churn_
data$total.intl.calls
```

We get four additional features by calculating the averages. This amounts to the inclusion of domain specific knowledge, which is that average usage per call could be a good feature.

We will now split the file into train and test set. The split will be 75 percent train and 25 percent test samples. We first create the `smp_size` variable, which is 75 percent of the number of rows in `churn_data`:

```
smp_size <- floor(0.75 * nrow(churn_data))
```

We next set the seed to make the partition reproducible. Each iteration will have the same split of data:

```
set.seed(123)
```

Then we sample 75 percent of the rows for training:

```
train_ind <- sample(seq_len(nrow(churn_data)), size = smp_size)
```

We create the train set using the sampled rows:

```
train <- churn_data[train_ind, ]
```

The test set is created by not selecting the previously selected rows:

```
test <- churn_data[-train_ind, ]
```

We see the distribution of churn and active accounts across the train and test sets:

```
table(train$Status)
```

The output of the `table` command, which shows the distribution of the target variable in the training dataset, is as follows:

```
False   True
3219    531
```

```
table(test$Status)
```

The output of the `table` command, which shows the distribution of the target variable in the test dataset, is as follows:

```
False   True
1074    176
```

The proportion of churn and active cases are similar in both the sets, hence we will use them. Otherwise, we would have changed the seed and rerun the split process until we got a similar proportion. The last step is to save the sets as csv files:

```
write.csv(train,file="churn_data_clean.all.csv",row.names = F)
write.csv(test,file="churn_data_clean_test.all.csv",row.names = F)
```

Later in this chapter we will be discussing customer segmentation. Let's prepare the data for customer segmentation, clustering algorithms only work with numeric data, so we need to discard categorical variables. For segmentation we intend to use only the features about time and number of calls during different parts of the day. We select columns 6 to 13 and write it to the file churn_cluster_data.csv.

```
churn_cluster_data<-churn_data[,6:13]
write.csv(churn_cluster_data,file="churn_cluster_data.csv",row.names = F)
```

Model training and validation

In the model training and validation phase, it's always a good idea to try multiple algorithms. We will try out OnlineLogisticRegression, AdaptiveLogisticRegression, and RandomForest for training the models. The idea is to see which algorithm works well for the data and select the best one.

Logistic regression

We need to clean the file to remove quotes and white spaces and replace NA introduced during the feature engineering phase with NA/0, which would be introduced if the numerator is zero. We will use the sed command with the inplace flag *-i* to preprocess the files. Please type the following command on the Linux terminal:

```
sed -i 's/"//g' churn_data_clean.all.csv
sed -i 's/NA/0/g' churn_data_clean.all.csv

sed -i 's/"//g' churn_data_clean_test.all.csv
sed -i 's/NA/0/g' churn_data_clean_test.all.csv
```

First, we will train using logistic regression:

```
mahout trainlogistic --input churn_data_clean.all.csv --output
logistic_model --target Status --predictors account.length area.code
international.plan voice.mail.plan number.vmail.messages total.day.
minutes total.day.calls total.eve.minutes total.eve.calls total.night.
minutes total.night.calls total.intl.minutes total.intl.calls number.
customer.service.calls avg.minute.day avg.minute.eve avg.minute.night
avg.minute.intl --types n w w w n n n n n n n n n n n n n n n --features 19
--passes 100 --rate 50 --categories 2
```

```
Status ~
4.392*Intercept Term + -0.259*account.length + 6.371*area.code=408 + 6.371*area.code=415 + 13.372*area.code=510 + 15.115*avg.minute.day + -187.
521*avg.minute.eve + 49.510*avg.minute.intl + 7.856*avg.minute.night + -187.780*international.plan=no + 12.248*international.plan=yes + 35.761*
number.customer.service.calls + -208.654*number.vmail.messages + 55.926*total.day.calls + 55.926*total.day.minutes + -208.654*total.eve.calls +
51.298*total.eve.minutes + -9.176*total.intl.calls + 54.310*total.intl.minutes + -187.521*total.night.calls + 35.761*total.night.minutes + -17
2.892*voice.mail.plan=no + -3.548*voice.mail.plan=yes
          Intercept Term 4.39244
          account.length -0.25912
          area.code=408 6.37142
          area.code=415 6.37142
          area.code=510 13.37247
          avg.minute.day 15.11525
          avg.minute.eve -187.52094
          avg.minute.intl 49.50975
          avg.minute.night 7.85579
 international.plan=no -187.78007
 international.plan=yes 12.24823
 number.customer.service.calls 35.76127
 number.vmail.messages -208.65359
          total.day.calls 55.92634
          total.day.minutes 55.92634
          total.eve.calls -208.65359
          total.eve.minutes 51.28983
          total.intl.calls -9.17570
          total.intl.minutes 54.31027
          total.night.calls -187.52094
          total.night.minutes 35.76127
          voice.mail.plan=no -172.89232
          voice.mail.plan=yes -3.54823
          54.310273351     -1.742775477     -0.259124306  -187.520940767  -208.653589241     -9.175698693     0.000000000     0.000000000     0.000000000
          0.000000000     35.761268860     -7.940675358    15.115248391    49.509745430      4.392440944    51.289831613    55.926342102     7.85578567
0   -1.484369175
```

Then, we test the model using `runlogistic`, and we check the AUC and confusion matrix over the training set:

```
mahout runlogistic --auc --confusion --input churn_data_clean.all.csv
--model logistic_model
```

```
AUC = 0.59
confusion: [[2856.0, 388.0], [363.0, 143.0]]
entropy: [[NaN, NaN], [-40.9, -17.5]]
```

Lastly, we check the performance over the test set:

```
mahout runlogistic --auc --confusion --input churn_data_clean_test.all.
csv  --model logistic_model
```

```
AUC = 0.61
confusion: [[949.0, 119.0], [125.0, 57.0]]
entropy: [[NaN, NaN], [-40.6, -20.7]]
```

The AUC and the confusion matrix are stable across the test and train sets, which means we have not overfitten the data.

Adaptive logistic regression

We use the `trainAdaptiveLogistic` command to train an ensemble of logistic regression. The configuration parameter passed is 100 passes over the data with 20 threads:

```
mahout trainAdaptiveLogistic --input churn_data_clean.all.csv --output
logistic_model --target Status --predictors account.length area.code
international.plan voice.mail.plan number.vmail.messages total.day.
minutes total.day.calls total.eve.minutes total.eve.calls total.night.
minutes total.night.calls total.intl.minutes total.intl.calls number.
customer.service.calls avg.minute.day avg.minute.eve avg.minute.night
avg.minute.intl --types n w w w n n n n n n n n n n n n n --features 19
--passes 100 --categories 2 --threads 20
```

```
Status ~
-23.607*account.length + -0.009*area.code=408 + -0.009*area.code=415 + -0.193*area.code=510 + -0.193*avg.mi
nute.day + -70.585*avg.minute.eve + -0.592*avg.minute.intl + -0.009*avg.minute.night + -94.192*internationa
l.plan=no + -0.009*international.plan=yes + 7.783*number.customer.service.calls + -139.634*number.vmail.mes
sages + 81.412*total.day.calls + 81.412*total.day.minutes + -139.634*total.eve.calls + -24.992*total.eve.mi
nutes + -1.145*total.intl.calls + -2.090*total.intl.minutes + -70.585*total.night.calls + 7.783*total.night
.minutes + -131.851*voice.mail.plan=no + 0.000*voice.mail.plan=yes
        account.length -23.60740
         area.code=408 -0.00906
         area.code=415 -0.00906
         area.code=510 -0.19301
        avg.minute.day -0.19302
        avg.minute.eve -70.58496
       avg.minute.intl -0.59216
      avg.minute.night -0.00910
international.plan=no -94.19237
international.plan=yes -0.00904
number.customer.service.calls 7.78292
number.vmail.messages -139.63350
        total.day.calls 81.41209
      total.day.minutes 81.41209
        total.eve.calls -139.63350
      total.eve.minutes -24.99213
        total.intl.calls -1.14452
      total.intl.minutes -2.08998
       total.night.calls -70.58496
     total.night.minutes 7.78292
      voice.mail.plan=no -131.85059
     voice.mail.plan=yes 0.00007
   -2.089983474    0.000009794    -23.607403892    -70.584962229    -139.633503742    -1.144523134    0.00000
```

The second step is to validate the model accuracy over the training dataset. We check the AUC and confusion matrix for this purpose:

```
mahout validateAdaptiveLogistic --input churn_data_clean.all.csv --model
logistic_model --auc --confusion
```

```
AUC = 0.39

=================================================
Confusion Matrix
- - - - - - - - - - - - - - - - - - - - - - - - - - - - - -
a         b         <--Classified as
3219      0         |  3219      a      = False
0         531       |  531       b      = True
```

The second step is to validate the model accuracy over the test dataset. We check the AUC and confusion matrix for this purpose:

```
mahout validateAdaptiveLogistic --input churn_data_clean_test.all.csv
--model logistic_model --auc --confusion
```

```
AUC = 0.39

=================================================
Confusion Matrix
- - - - - - - - - - - - - - - - - - - - - - - - - - - - - -
a         b         <--Classified as
1074      0         |  1074      a      = False
0         176       |  176       b      = True
```

Random forest

As the random forest implementation in Mahout doesn't work with the header line, we remove the header. We will use sed for this purpose:

```
sed -i '1d' churn_data_clean.all.csv
sed -i '1d' churn_data_clean_test.all.csv
```

The next step is to create a directory on HDFS and copy the files to this HDFS directory:

```
hadoop fs -mkdir chapter9
hadoop fs -put churn_data_clean.all.csv chapter9
hadoop fs -put churn_data_clean_test.all.csv chapter9
```

The next step is to create the description file. We create it in the hdfs folder created previously:

```
hadoop jar $MAHOUT_HOME/mahout-core-0.9-job.jar org.apache.mahout.
classifier.df.tools.Describe -p chapter9/churn_data_clean.all.csv -f
chapter9/churn.info -d 1 n 3 c 10 n 1 4 n
```

Then we proceed to train the model. We will build 100 trees in the forest:

```
hadoop jar $MAHOUT_HOME/mahout-examples-0.9-job.jar org.apache.mahout.
classifier.df.mapreduce.BuildForest -Dmapred.max.split.size=1874231 -d
chapter9/churn_data_clean.all.csv -ds chapter9/churn.info -sl 4 -p -t 100
-o chapter9_final-forest
```

The last step is to test the model's performance over test and train sets:

```
hadoop jar $MAHOUT_HOME/mahout-examples-0.9-job.jar org.apache.mahout.
classifier.df.mapreduce.TestForest -i chapter9/churn_data_clean.all.
csv -ds chapter9/churn.info -m chapter9_final-forest -a -mr -o chapter9_
final-pred
```

```
Summary
-------------------------------------------------
Correctly Classified Instances          :      3682      98.1867%
Incorrectly Classified Instances        :        68       1.8133%
Total Classified Instances              :      3750


=================================================
Confusion Matrix
-------------------------------------------------
a        b      <--Classified as
463      68      |  531         a     = True
0        3219    |  3219        b     = False


=================================================
Statistics
-------------------------------------------------
Kappa                                   0.9182
Accuracy                                98.1867%
Reliability                             62.398%
Reliability (standard deviation)        0.5442
```

We repeat the last step with the test dataset and check the performance of the model:

```
hadoop jar $MAHOUT_HOME/mahout-examples-0.9-job.jar org.apache.mahout.
classifier.df.mapreduce.TestForest -i chapter9/churn_data_clean_test.all.
csv -ds chapter9/churn.info -m chapter9_final-forest -a -mr -o chapter9_
final-pred_test
```

```
==================================================
Summary
--------------------------------------------------
Correctly Classified Instances      :     1180        94.4%
Incorrectly Classified Instances    :       70         5.6%
Total Classified Instances          :     1250

==================================================
Confusion Matrix
--------------------------------------------------
a       b       <--Classified as
116     60      |   176          a     = True
10      1064    |   1074         b     = False

==================================================
Statistics
--------------------------------------------------
Kappa                                    0.7296
Accuracy                                 94.4%
Reliability                              54.9927%
Reliability (standard deviation)         0.5043
```

Out of the three algorithms, RandomForest has the best performance. We can
further tune the models by adjusting the parameters and observing the results.
For RandomForest, we can change the values of -*t* (number of trees) and -*sl*
(number of features used per tree) to choose the best model.

Customer segmentation

The next analytics use case that we are going to discuss is customer segmentation.
Customer segmentation is the process of dividing and grouping customers into
meaningful subgroups or segments according to some notion of similarity. Segments
are separated by natural boundaries in the data. Customer segmentation allows an
organization to better understand their customer base and build different strategies
based on the segments observed. For example, consider a hypothetical scenario:
a telecom service provider segments subscribers based on their age, voice usage,
and data usage, and after segmentation might observe five distinct segments.
The segments are shown in the following table:

Segments	Age	Voice Usage	Data Usage
Segment A	Old	High	Low
Segment B	Old	Low	Low
Segment C	Middle Age	High	High
Segment D	Young	High	Low
Segment E	Young	Low	High

Now the subscriber, based on this information, can decide different campaigns for each segment, thus getting greater returns for his marketing expense.

There are many different types of customer segmentation. We will briefly discuss a few of them:

- **Value-based segmentation**: Any customer or subscriber is associated with a value. The subscriber value can be measured in different ways and may have different terms associated with it. It could either be the license fee amount or annual recurring revenue or customer lifetime value. To identify the most valued customers or to track value changes over time, value-based segmentation is used. The customers are grouped together according to their value.

- **Behavioral-based segmentation**: Behavioral-based segmentation is done on product ownership and adoption or utilization data. Customers are grouped according to their product usage pattern. This type of segmentation is very useful for customizing the product offering, coming up with new features, and so on.

- **Demographic-based segmentation**: This type of segmentation is aimed at discovering different customer groupings based on socio-demographic aspects such as age, income, marital status, and so on.

In this case study, we are going to focus on behavioral segmentation based on telecom usage. The dataset would be the same as the one used for the churn analytics but we will use only numeric features.

Preprocessing

For a segmentation project, the data needs to be preprocessed. There are two common ways of preprocessing the data, by normalization and by rescaling it. Both are introduced as follows:

- Rescale: Scaling each entry of a feature between 0 and 1
- Normalize: Making every feature zero mean, unit variance

For behavioral segmentation, it is important to have an understanding of the behavior we are interested in segmenting for. In this case, we could be interested in understanding the behavior according to the time of the call (day, evening, or night), type of call (international or voice mail), and so on. The data representation for each of the cases will depend upon the behavior we are interested, in as we will see in the section ahead.

There is a lot of value in exploratory clustering too, but without a clear objective in mind it is a bit difficult to interpret the clusters. Generally, you play with different cluster numbers and feature representation and then try to interpret each good result.

Feature extraction

We will consider a few usecases of behavior-based clustering. In all these cases, we will consider internal and external evaluation metrics to check the efficacy of the segments. The internal evaluation metrics used will be inter and intra-cluster distances and for external evaluation we will churn the *Status* label feature.

Day calls

The first behavior we will be interested in observing is the behavior according to the calls made during the day. The first step is to cluster the subscriber based on the features mentioned in the table and then try to find some interesting patterns. Once the clusters are satisfactory, the next step is to see how the observation variables behave across clusters, in this case, we have the churn label, *Status*, as the observational variable and we will check the count of the two categories of the variables *Status*, *True*, and *False* across the different clusters. The feature related to day calls are mentioned in the following table:

Features
total.day.minutes
total.day.calls

Evening calls

We are going to repeat the same steps discussed previously for evening calls and international calls. We will cluster them separately and then compute the count of the two different values for the *Status* field. The features related to evening calls are mentioned in the following table:

Features
total.eve.minutes
total.eve.calls

International calls

Similarly, the international calls dataset will have *total.intl.minutes* and *total.intl.calls* as the features and are mentioned in the following table:

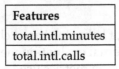

Features
total.intl.minutes
total.intl.calls

Preprocessing the files

We first need to preprocess the files to create the sequence files and the initial centroids. We need to remove the header line and replace commas with space so that we can use the preprocessing code from *Chapter 7, Clustering with Mahout*:

```
sed -i '1d' churn_cluster_data.csv
sed -i 's/,/ /g' churn_cluster_data.csv
```

Next we create the HDFS directory chapter09 on Hadoop and copy the file to the directory.

```
hadoop fs -mkdir chapter09/clustering_input
hadoop fs -put churn_cluster_data.csv chapter09/clustering_input/
```

Now open the file DataPreprocessing.java from the package chapter7.src, we need to change the path to the input directory and run the code.

```
//create the configuration object and add resources
Configuration conf = new Configuration();
conf.addResource(new Path("/usr/local/hadoop/conf/core-site.xml"));
conf.addResource(new Path("/usr/local/hadoop/conf/hdfs-site.xml"));

//create the file system object and pass the configuration object
FileSystem fileSystem = FileSystem.get(conf);
```

We then create the input and output Path objects.

```
#define the input and sequence file directory
```

We need to change the path of the input directory from chapter7/clustering/input to chapter7/clustering/input. Once we have made the changes, the paths will look like the following code:

```
String inputPath="chapter09/clustering_input";
String inputSeq="clustering_seq";

Path inputDir = new Path(inputPath);
Path inputSeqDir = new Path(inputSeq);
```

```
//The last step is to encode the vectors using the //
RandomAccessSparseVector
InputDriver.runJob(inputDir, inputSeqDir,          "org.apache.mahout.
math.RandomAccessSparseVector",conf);
```

Creating the clusters using fuzzy k-means

Once the files have been processed, we will use the Mahout fkmeans command to cluster them together. We could try different clustering algorithms as discussed previously; that can be as an exercise. We will create three clusters:

```
mahout fkmeans -i clustering_seq -c chapter09/kmeans_init_cluster -o
chapter09/clustering_output_fkmeans -dm org.apache.mahout.common.
distance.EuclideanDistanceMeasure -x 10 -k 3 -ow --clustering -m 1.2
```

Once the clustering step is completed, we will observe the output.

Check the following files in the output directory:

```
hadoop fs -ls chapter09/clustering_output_fkmeans
```

```
/user/ctiwary/chapter09/clustering_output_fkmeans/_policy
/user/ctiwary/chapter09/clustering_output_fkmeans/clusteredPoints
/user/ctiwary/chapter09/clustering_output_fkmeans/clusters-0
/user/ctiwary/chapter09/clustering_output_fkmeans/clusters-/user/ctiwary/
chapter09/clustering_output_fkmeans/clusters-/user/ctiwary/chapter09/
clustering_output_fkmeans/clusters-3-final
```

To check the cluster centroids, we will use the clusterdump utility:

```
mahout clusterdump -i chapter09/clustering_output_fkmeans/clusters-*-final
```

Clustering using k-means

The next clustering algorithm that we are going to try is kmeans with three clusters. We will use the kmeans command of the Mahout command line utility:

```
mahout kmeans -i clustering_seq -c chapter09/kmeans_init_cluster -o
chapter09/clustering_output -dm org.apache.mahout.common.distance.
EuclideanDistanceMeasure -x 10 -k 3 -ow --clustering
```

Evaluation

We will use Mahout's implementation for internal cluster evaluation. Cluster evaluation requires passing a distance measure. We will create the distance measure object as follows:

```
//create the distance measure object
DistanceMeasure measure = new EuclideanDistanceMeasure();
```

We run the `RepresentativePointsDriver.run` method that sets up the `ClusterEvaluator` object properties:

```
RepresentativePointsDriver.run(conf, new Path("chapter09/clustering_
output_fkmeans/clusters-3-final"),
new Path("chapter09/clustering_output", " chapter09/clusteredPoints"),
new Path("chapter09/clustering_output_fkmeans"),measure,
10, true);
```

Then we create the `ClusterEvaluator` object and pass the `Configuration` object and path to the cluster output directory:

```
ClusterEvaluator cv = new ClusterEvaluator(conf,new Path("chapter09/
clustering_output/clusters-3-final"));
```

We call the respective functions to calculate the inter-cluster and intra-cluster density of the clusters:

```
System.out.println(cv.interClusterDensity());
System.out.println(cv.intraClusterDensity());
```

We can calculate the evaluation metrics for other clustering algorithms too, using the same methodology.

Summary

In this chapter, we discussed the end-to-end steps involved in a machine learning project, taking two common customer analytics use cases, churn analytics and customer segmentation, as examples. We considered structured data for building the models. Many of the techniques learned up until now where put into practice. We discussed data cleansing, feature engineering, and model efficacy. A robust and repeatable step-by-step plan, which puts equal importance on all phases of a machine learning project, is important to its success.

In the last chapter, we will continue with the same theme and discuss text analytics use cases. Text analytics is an example of using unstructured data to gain insight and build models. We will cover the end-to-end steps that need to be performed to analyze text. The use cases that will be covered are text clustering and classification.

10
Case Study – Text Analytics

So far, we have focused on deriving insights and building models on top of data that has a well defined and fixed structure. Data sources such as delimited files and database tables have a fixed format and are called structured sources of data. Structured data is the mainstay of analytics, and most of the use cases we discussed rely on structured data. Data sources such as social media posts, support case comments, e-mails, articles, and so on are called unstructured, data and they can contain business insights about customers and products that is not readily available in structured data. For example, structured information such as product usage tables can tell us that a particular customer is not using the product, but the reason for that could be documented in a support case comment. Mining unstructured data for information follows a slightly different approach than what we have discussed so far. In this chapter, we are going to discuss the steps involved in a text analytics project as a use case of mining unstructured data. You will understand the vector space model of representing text and run clustering and classification algorithms on it. The topics covered in this chapter are as follows:

- Vector space model
- Text clustering
- Text classification
- Feature extraction

Text analytics

Text analytics has many practical applications and is one of the most important areas of application of machine learning. Automatic e-mail filters, news article clustering and categorization, and sentimental analysis on social media posts about products are some of the most widely implemented use cases of text analytics. One of the major challenges in text analytics is feature extraction. Representation of documents is the most critical part of a text analytics project. In the coming sections, we are going to discuss one of the most-used forms of representation of text.

Vector space model

The representation of a set of documents as vectors in a common vector space is known as the **vector space model (VSM)**, and it is commonly used in many text analytics problem, such as topic modelling, document classification, and document clustering. The VSM is a common and prominent way of vectorizing text documents.

In the vector space model, each unique word present in the set of documents is represented as a coordinate of a vector. If we imagine a matrix, each column of the matrix will represent a word, and each row will be a document of the document set. The value of the matrix cells will indicate whether a word is present in a document, and a sense of how frequent the occurrence is. The dimensionality of such a matrix will be very high.

For example, let's assume we have two documents, A and B. A has the `This is document A and this is the first document` text, and B has the `This is document B and this is the second document` text. We will consider the simplest form of vector space model; each word is indexed, and we are going to fill the cell values with simple counts. There are other more intelligent ways of creating a VSM and we will discuss that in later sections. As we parse the documents, we see that there are 11 unique words; each will become a column in the matrix.

Document	this	is	document	A	B	and	the	first	second
A	2	2	2	1	0	1	1	1	0
B	2	2	2	0	1	1	1	0	1

A cursory look at the VSM can provide some interesting pointers. One thing we notice is that words such as "this", "is", "and", and so on are not very important, as they are common across all documents. A feature-like "Document" could be interesting, but as we see the counts are the same, maybe we need to look at other ways of presenting the data that could be more interesting. Words such as "A", "B", "first", and "second" are definitely important words. In later sections, we will discuss how these initial pointers lead to some important feature extraction techniques.

The vector space model process can be divided into three broad stages:

- The first step is the preprocessing of raw textual information.

- The second step is document indexing, where content-bearing terms, unique words present in text, are extracted from the document text.

- The third step is the weighting of the indexed terms, for example TF/IDF, to enhance retrieval of the document relevant to the current problem.

Preprocessing

Before we can analyze and index documents in the vector space model, the text needs to be preprocessed. We will discuss some of the most common preprocessing tasks. It's better to use purpose-built tools such as Tika and Lucene for parsing and preprocessing the documents, instead of writing our own implementation. We will discuss an example based on Lucene later on. Let's now look at some common preprocessing tasks. They are presented in the order in which they should be performed.

Tokenization

The first task that needs to be performed in preprocessing of text is to tokenize each document. Tokenization refers to the process of extracting words from the document text. In this process, we have to handle cases such as white spaces, bad characters, special words such as e-mails, and so on. All words need to be converted to lowercase.

Stop word removal

We saw in the example of the vector space model that some common words such as "a", "and", "this", and so on are not very predictive and lead to noise. These words are called stop words and should be removed.

Stemming

Stemming is the process of converting a word into its root form. Words such as "kick" and "kicking" in most cases should be treated as the same. Performing stemming takes care of this requirement.

Preprocessing example

Open the `PreprocessDataExample.java` file from the `chapter10.src` package present in the code repository that comes with this book. This file contains an example of preprocessing text using Lucene analyzer. You will learn how to create your own analyzer that includes tokenizing text, stop word removal, lowercase filtering, and stemming.

We define a function, `displayTokenUsingStandardAnalyzer()`, to accomplish the aforementioned preprocessing task:

```
private static void displayTokenUsingStandardAnalyzer() throws
IOException {
String text = "Lucene is simple but yet a powerful Java based at search
library. StandardAnalyzer will convert all words to lowercase and remove
stop words";
Analyzer analyzer = new StandardAnalyzer(Version.LUCENE_46);
```

```
TokenStream tokenStream = analyzer.tokenStream(null, new StringReader(
text));

tokenStream.reset();
while (tokenStream.incrementToken()) {
System.out.println(tokenStream
.getAttribute(CharTermAttribute.class).toString());
}
tokenStream.close();
System.out.println("Stemmimg Example \n");
String text_stem = "Lucene is simple but yet a powerful Java based at
search library. This is to check stemming by PorterStemFilter, kicking
will become kick";
tokenStream = analyzer.tokenStream(null, new StringReader(text_stem));
tokenStream = new PorterStemFilter(tokenStream);
tokenStream.reset();
while (tokenStream.incrementToken()) {
System.out.println(tokenStream
.getAttribute(CharTermAttribute.class).toString());
}
tokenStream.close();
analyzer.close();
}
```

At the start of the function, we defined a string variable with the name `text`.
The string variable will be used to demonstrate the text processing. Then we
created the `StandardAnalyzer` object. `StandardAnalyzer` is an out-of-the-box
analyzer in Lucene that performs removal of white spaces, tokenization of words,
converting all tokens to lowercase, and removing stop words. The `text` string
variable is processed using `StandardAnalyzer`, and the output is as follows:

```
Example with Sandard Analyzer

lucene
simple
yet
powerful
java
based
search
library
standardanalyzer
convert
all
words
lowercase
remove
stop
words
```

We can see that all the words have become lowercase, whitespaces have been removed, and stop words such as "a", "at", and so on have been removed. Now we will add a filter to the standard analyzer to augment its capabilities. A filter is an additional operation we would want to perform on the data. We should also stem the words to their root form. We add the `PorterStemFilter` filter to the `analyzer` object. `PorterStemFilter` stems words in English to their root form. The `text_stem` variable is used to test the implementation. The output looks like what is shown in this screenshot:

```
Example after the inclusion of stemmimg of words

lucen
simpl
yet
power
java
base
search
librari
check
stem
porterstemfilt
kick
becom
kick
```

We can see that many words have been stemmed; for example, "kicking" is stemmed to "kick". We will use the building blocks from this example to build our own custom analyzer in the sections ahead.

Document indexing

After preprocessing has been completed, the next step is to perform document indexing. After document indexing, we get the matrix discussed in the vector space model. There are many ways to compute the cell values. One of the simplest is **term frequency** (**TF**). The cell values are populated with the count of the particular word or term in a particular document. This is required because, even after removing the stop words, there may be some words that would be common across most documents. These words will not help us distinguish different documents. On the other hand, words that are common in a set of documents but not common otherwise in all the documents might be very important. We need to take this into account while indexing the document. We will discuss this technique in the next section, called term weighting.

TF-IDF weighting

Term frequency-inverse document frequency (TF-IDF) index weighting scheme is an improvement on term frequency weighting aimed at finding out the most common words in a document but penalising for common words present across documents. For example documents on political ideology will have the words 'politics' common across all documents and shouldn't be considered very important. Multiplication by inverse document frequency, the number of documents a word is present in, reduces the value of frequently occurring words across documents compared to the importance of infrequent words.

Let's revisit the previous example; we have removed the stop words.

The term frequency of words is as follows:

Document	document	A	B	first	second
A	2	1	0	1	0
B	2	0	1	0	1

The document frequency of words is the number of documents the word is present in, as shown in the following table:

Document	document	A	B	first	second
A	2	1	1	1	1

TF-IDF is the multiplication of the term frequency with the inverse, $1/DF$, of the document frequency:

Document	document	A	B	first	second
A	1	1	0	1	0
B	1	0	1	0	1

A variation of TF-IDF is to multiply the product by the number of documents, N. The formula would be given by $TFIDF = TF*1/DF*N$. Another variation is to take the logarithm of DF and multiply it by TF.

n-grams

A group of words in a sequence is called an n-gram. The intuition behind creating n-grams is that certain words make sense when considered together, for example "social media". A single word iscan be called a unigram, and two words a, such as "Coca Cola", can be considered a single unit and called a bigram, three a trigram and so onm. Combinations of three and more terms can be called trigrams, 4-grams, 5-grams, and so on.

Classic TF-IDF weighting assumes that words occur independent ofiDF of other words, but vectors created using this method usually lack the ability to identify key features of documents, which may be dependentThis is different from the classic TF-IDF approach of treating term as independent of each other and is an improvement as it can capture the dependency between terms.

Some of these can be good combinations for generating document vectors ("big bang", "the best ever"), but some of them aren't ("a" and "the").The n-grams generated can also be significant, like "social media" or insignificant like "a big" Hyou combine the unigrams and bigrams from a document and generate weights using TF-IDF, you'll end up with, also many infrequent but meaningless n-bigrams will be generated that havethat have large weightslarge weights because of their largetheir large IDF. This is undesirable To address this issue.

We can solve this problem by passing then-grams through something called awe can use the log-likelihoodLog-likelihood test on the n-grams. The test will retain the significant n-grams and weed out the insignificant and infrequent ones. It can determine whether two words occurred together by chance or because they form a significant unit. It selects the most significant n-grams and prunes away the least significant n-grams. Using the remaining n-grams, the TF-IDF weighting scheme is applied and vectors are produced. In this way, significant bigrams such as "Coca Cola" can be more properly accounted for in a TF-IDF weighting.

Normalization

The document is large, and its vector has many nonzero dimensions, causing it to be close to many smaller documents. Somehow, we need to negate the effect of varying sizes of the vectors when calculating similarity. This process of decreasing the magnitude of large vectors and increasing the magnitude of smaller vectors is called normalization. Normalization is used to make instances and features comparable. In the case of text mining it is used handle extreme-cases which can skew the results, for example to make documents of different sizes comparable. Larger documents are less sparse and can match up with many different smaller documents. We can address this by penalizing the vectors by its length.

In Mahout, normalization uses what is known in statistics asap-norm.Mahout supports different forms on normalization using the norm of a vector, T the p-norm of a vector x is given by this formula:

$$|x|_p \equiv \left(\sum_i |x_i|^p \right)^{1/p}$$

The parameterThe parameter p could should be any valuea value greater than 0. For example tThe 1-norm, or Manhattan norm, of a vector is the vector divided by the sum of the weights of all the dimensions.

The 2-norm, also commonly known as Euclidean norm ornorm or the L2-norm, is the vector divided by the magnitude of the vector-this magnitude which is the length of the vector, as we're accustomed to understanding it: and is given by the following formula:

$$\left| x \right|_2 = \left| x \right| = \sqrt{x_1^2 + x_2^2 + \ldots + x_2^2}$$

The infinite norm is simply the vector divided by the weight of the largest magnitude dimension.

The norm power (*p*) you choose will depend on the type of operations done on the vector. If the distance measure used is the Manhattan distance measure, the 1-norm will often yield better results with the data. Similarly, if the cosine of the Euclidean distance measure is being used to calculate similarity, the 2-norm version of the vectors yields better results. For best results, the normalization should relate to the notion of distance used in the similarity metrics.

Generating the 2-normalized bigram vector is done by running the Mahout launcher using the `seq2sparse` command, with the –n flag set to 2:

```
mahout seq2sparse -i reuters-seqfiles/ -o reuters-normalized-bigram -ow
-a org.apache.lucene.analysis.WhitespaceAnalyzer
-chunk 200 -wt tfidf -s 5 -md 3 -x 90 -ng 2 -ml 50 -seq -n 2
```

Normalization improves the quality of clustering a little. Further refinement in the quality of clustering is achieved by using problem-specific distance measures and appropriate algorithms.

Clustering text

The clustering of text has many applications. It deals with grouping similar documents based on the words present in the text. One of the most common examples would be the clustering of news articles into similar groups. We will discuss how to implement the clustering of text using Mahout.

The dataset

We will be using `Reuters` dataset for the clustering example. This dataset has a repository of e-mails. We will download the dataset and then extract it using `tar` to the `reuters-sgm` folder. Move to the directory `data/chapter10` and execute the following commands:

```
export MAHOUT_LOCAL=TRUE
curl http://kdd.ics.uci.edu/databases/reuters21578/reuters21578.tar.gz -o
reuters21578.tar.gz

mkdir -p reuters-sgm

tar xzf reuters21578.tar.gz -C reuters-sgm
```

We will use Mahout's inbuilt utility to extract the `Reuters` dataset into the `reuters-out` folder:

```
mahout org.apache.lucene.benchmark.utils.ExtractReuters reuters-sgm
reuters-out
```

The last step is to convert the file into a sequence file using Mahout's `seqdirectory` command:

```
mahout seqdirectory -i reuters-out -o reuters-out-seqdir -c UTF-8 -chunk
64 -xm sequential
```

Feature extraction

Open the `TextPreprocessingExample.java` file from the `chapter10.src` package present in the code repository that comes with this book. This code file reads the input sequence file, uses a custom analyzer to tokenize and preprocess the text, and creates the TF-IDF vectors.

We first create the path variables for the input and output directories and then declare the custom analyzer:

```
String inputDir = "data/chapter10/reuters-out-seqdir";
Configuration conf = new Configuration();
String outputDir = "data/chapter10/reuters-features";
Path tokenizedPath = new Path(outputDir,
DocumentProcessor.TOKENIZED_DOCUMENT_OUTPUT_FOLDER);
System.out.println(tokenizedPath);
CustomAnalyzer analyzer = new CustomAnalyzer();
DocumentProcessor.tokenizeDocuments(new Path(inputDir), analyzer
.getClass().asSubclass(Analyzer.class), tokenizedPath, conf);
```

The input and output directory path is taken as the input from the user, and we create the `CustomAnalyzer` object. The `CustomAnalyzer` object is used to tokenize the text document. Open the `CustomAnalyzer.java` file from the `chapter10.src` package present in the code repository that comes with this book. This code file contains the implementation of the custom analyzer. This analyzer performs the same operations as we saw in the previous example as it removes whitespaces and stop words, tokenizes words, converts words to lowercase, and stems the words:

```
public class CustomAnalyzer extends Analyzer {

@Override
public TokenStreamComponents createComponents(String field, Reader
reader) {
Tokenizer source = new StandardTokenizer(Version.LUCENE_46,reader);
StandardAnalyzer analyzer = new StandardAnalyzer(Version.LUCENE_46);
TokenStream filter;
try {
filter = analyzer.tokenStream(field,reader);
} catch (IOException e) {
e.printStackTrace();
}
filter = new PorterStemFilter(source);
analyzer.close();
return new TokenStreamComponents(source, filter);
}
}
```

A custom analyzer needs to extend the analyzer class and override the `createComponents()` method. In our implementation, we create a `Tokenizer` object and a `StandardAnalyzer` object, create a `TokenStream` object and a `PorterStemFilter` object, and then return a `TokenStreamComponents` object with `Tokenizer` and `TokenStream` objects as the arguments to the constructor.

Once the text is tokenized, we need to create the term frequency vector:

```
DictionaryVectorizer.createTermFrequencyVectors(tokenizedPath,
new Path(outputDir), tfDirName, conf, minSupport, maxNGramSize,
minLLRValue, norm, logNormalize, reduceTasks, chunkSize,
sequentialAccessOutput, namedVectors);
```

The `createTermFrequencyVectors()` method of the `DictionaryVectorizer` class takes as arguments the path to the tokenized directory, the output directory, and a bunch of arguments regarding how to create the term frequency vector.

Then we need to calculate the document frequency of each token. The `calculateDF()` function of `TFIDFConverter` does that for us. We store the document frequencies in the `docFrequenciesFeatures` variable:

```
docFrequenciesFeatures = TFIDFConverter.calculateDF(new Path(outputDir,
tfDirName), new Path(outputDir), conf, chunkSize);
```

The next step is to prune the tokens with high document frequencies. This is done by the `pruneVectors()` method of the `HighDFWordsPruner` class:

```
HighDFWordsPruner.pruneVectors(tfDir, prunedTFDir, prunedPartialTFDir,
maxDFThreshold, minDf, conf, docFrequenciesFeatures, -1.0f,
false, reduceTasks);
```

The last step is to calculate the TF-IDF and save the output. This task is performed by the `processTfIdf()` function of the `TFIDFConverter` class. The major arguments for the function `processTfIdf()` are as follows:

- `Input`: This is the input directory of the vectors in the SequenceFile format.
- `Output`: This is the output directory in which the document are generated.
- `datasetFeatures`: Information about document frequencies.
- `minDf`: The minimum document frequency. Default value is 1.
- `maxDF`: This is the maximum percentage of vectors for the DF. Default value is 99.
- `NumReducers`: The number of reducers to be used by the job.

The `processTfIdf()` function is called by passing the respective arguments:

```
TFIDFConverter.processTfIdf(new Path(outputDir,
DictionaryVectorizer.DOCUMENT_VECTOR_OUTPUT_FOLDER), new Path(
outputDir), conf, docFrequenciesFeatures, minDf, maxDFPercent,
norm, logNormalize, sequentialAccessOutput, namedVectors,
reduceTasks);
```

The TF-IDF vectors created can be used for both clustering and classification of text. We will discuss this in the next sections.

The clustering job

Open the `KMeansClusteringExample.java` file from the `chapter10.src` package present in the code repository that comes with this book. The code file includes an example of clustering using `Kmeans` and evaluation of the cluster using inter cluster and intra cluster distance as a metric.

The first step is to declare the output directory, input vector folder, path to initial centroids and the `Configuration` object:

```
String outputDir = "data/chapter10/reuters-features";
Path vectorsFolder = new Path(outputDir, "tfidf-vectors");
Path centroids = new Path(outputDir, "centroids");
Path clusterOutput = new Path(outputDir, "clusters");
Configuration conf = new Configuration();
```

Then we create the initial cluster centroid. We will use `CosineDistanceMeasure` for the measure of similarity, and the number of clusters will be 20. For text mining, the preferred distance measure is `CosineDistanceMeasure`, an important advantage being that it can account for documents of different sizes:

```
RandomSeedGenerator.buildRandom(conf, vectorsFolder, centroids, 20,
new CosineDistanceMeasure());
```

Once the cluster centroids are created, we pass them along with the declared directories to the `KMeansDriver` run method to build the clusters:

```
KMeansDriver.run(conf, vectorsFolder, centroids, clusterOutput, 0.01,
20, true, 0, false);
```

Once the clustering is complete, we need to evaluate it. We declare the distance measure, which should be the same as that used by the clustering algorithm. Then we call the `RepresentativePointsDriver` run() method:

```
CosineDistanceMeasure measure = new CosineDistanceMeasure();

RepresentativePointsDriver.run(conf, new Path(clusterOutput,"clusters-10-
final"), new Path(
clusterOutput, "clusteredPoints"), clusterOutput, measure, 20, true);
```
The next step is to create the ClusterEvaluator object and measure the inter and intra cluster density:
```
ClusterEvaluator cv = new ClusterEvaluator(conf,new
Path(clusterOutput,"clusters-10-final"));

System.out.println(cv.interClusterDensity());

System.out.println(cv.intraClusterDensity());
```

Categorizing text

Text categorization or classification deals with labeling documents to certain predefined classes. One of the most common tasks of text classification is labeling e-mail as ham and spam. We will discuss how to implement text classification in Mahout.

The dataset

For the text classification case study, we are going to use the `20 newsgroups` dataset. The data is from transcripts of several months of postings made in 20 Usenet newsgroups on 20 different topics. Download the dataset from `http://people.csail.mit.edu/jrennie/20Newsgroups/20news-bydate.tar.gz`.

The dataset is divided into train and test sets, and each set has 20 subdirectories. If you look at the training folder, you will see these 20 subdirectories. Each subdirectory will be considered a class label, and all files belonging to the directory will belong to that class. The following screenshot displays the folders in which files of respective classes as present. The folder name is the class label for documents present inside it.

Let's look at the file in the `alt.atheism` directory. We will look at the `53314` file.

```
From: cjhs@minster.york.ac.uk
Subject: Re: free moral agency
Distribution: world
Organization: Department of Computer Science, University of York, England
Lines: 11

: Are you saying that their was a physical Adam and Eve, and that all
: humans are direct decendents of only these two human beings.?  Then who
: were Cain and Able's wives?  Couldn't be their sisters, because A&E
: didn't have daughters.  Were they non-humans?

Genesis 5:4

and the days of Adam after he begat Seth were eight hundred years, and
he begat sons and daughters:

Felicitations -- Chris Ho-Stuart
~
```

The file has a header section with information such as the sender of the e-mail, the subject line, number of lines in the message, and so on. Then we have the message body.

Feature extraction

The important features in this data will be in the headers and the message body. Counts of words in the header, most frequent words in the header, number of lines in messages, and words in the message body are some of the important features to look out. We will discuss feature extraction and training a classifier in the next section.

The classification job

Open the `ClassificationExamples.java` file from the `chapter10.src` package present in the code repository that comes with this book. In this code file, we will extract the features, encode them as vectors, and train a classification model to classify documents to respective class labels.

Let's discuss the code now. At first, we define the number of features to be used for training and the path to the input training directory:

```
private static final int FEATURES = 10000;
File base = new File("data/chapter10/20news-bydate/20news-bydate-train");
```

Then we declare the vector encoding of the features that we derive from the messages. We declare separate encoders for the message body, intercept term, and header lines:

```
Map<String, Set<Integer>> traceDictionary = new TreeMap<String,
Set<Integer>>();
FeatureVectorEncoder encoder = new StaticWordValueEncoder("body");
encoder.setProbes(2);
encoder.setTraceDictionary(traceDictionary);
FeatureVectorEncoder bias = new ConstantValueEncoder("Intercept");
bias.setTraceDictionary(traceDictionary);
FeatureVectorEncoder lines = new ConstantValueEncoder("Lines");
lines.setTraceDictionary(traceDictionary);
```

We define the `OnlineLogisticRegression` object with categories set to `20`. Each category corresponds to one subdirectory in the `20news-bydate-train` directory. The OnlineLogisticRegression constructor accepts arguments, specifying the total number of categories in the target variable, the dimensions of the feature vectors, and an object of a regularizer, for example L1 or L2.

Different configuration arguments can be passed to the learning algorithm. The `alpha`, `decayExponent`, and `stepOffset` methods control the rate and method by which the learning rate varies. The lambda method specifies the amount of regularization, and the `learningRate` method specifies the initial learning rate of the algorithm:

```
OnlineLogisticRegression learningAlgorithm =
new OnlineLogisticRegression(
20, FEATURES, new L1())
.alpha(1).stepOffset(1000)
.decayExponent(0.9)
.lambda(3.0e-5)
.learningRate(20);
```

In the next step, we parse the `20news-bydate-train` directory and read the filename and the file list. The collection is shuffled to maintain the randomness so that the model sees the training example:

```
List<File> files = new ArrayList<File>();
for (File newsgroup : base.listFiles()) {
newsGroups.intern(newsgroup.getName());
files.addAll(Arrays.asList(newsgroup.listFiles()));

}


Collections.shuffle(files);
System.out.printf("%d training files\n", files.size());
```

The next step is to loop through each file in the subdirectory, extract the features and the target label, encode the features into vectors, and train the regression model.

The following code snippet creates the target label in the `actual` variable :

```
BufferedReader reader = new BufferedReader(new FileReader(file));
String ng = file.getParentFile().getName();
int actual = newsGroups.intern(ng);
```

The average line count of messages per target class is created:

```
String line = reader.readLine();
while (line != null && line.length() > 0) {
if (line.startsWith("Lines:")) {
//String count =
try {
lineCount = line.split(":",1).length;
averageLineCount += (lineCount - averageLineCount)
/ Math.min(k + 1, 1000);
} catch (NumberFormatException e) {
lineCount = averageLineCount;
}
}
```

Next, the features are encoded in vectors and prepared for training:

```
Vector v = new RandomAccessSparseVector(FEATURES);
bias.addToVector("", 1, v);
lines.addToVector("", lineCount / 30, v);
logLines.addToVector("", Math.log(lineCount + 1), v);
for (String word : words.elementSet()) {
encoder.addToVector(word, Math.log(1 + words.count(word)), v);
}
```

The prepared vector is used for training with the target label. This is done for each of the files:

```
learningAlgorithm.train(actual, v);
```

The `learningAlgorithm` trained model can be used to label a new dataset. The object has more than one method to perform the classification, for example function `trainAll()`. We have demonstrated one of them; the others can be checked in the online documentation at `http://mahout.apache.org/`.

The `classify()` function computes and returns a vector containing n-1 scores, where n is equal to `numCategories()`, given an input vector instance. Higher scores indicate that the input vector is more likely to belong to that category:

```
learningAlgorithm.classify(v);
```

Summary

This is the last chapter of this book. We discussed the fundamental concepts and an implementation of two major use cases of text analytics in Mahout. Throughout this book, we discussed the major concepts of machine learning, its implementation, and its usage in Mahout. This will give you a strong foundation for building a career in data analytics. I hope this book fulfilled its objective of providing a kick start in machine learning and Mahout, and I hope you continue building on and improving your skills.

Index

URL, for dataset 133
user neighborhood
  about 132
  fixed size neighborhood 133
  threshold-based neighborhood 133

V

validation
  about 29
  holdout-set validation 29
  K-fold cross validation 29
value-based segmentation 198
vector
  about 169
  arithmetic operations, performing 170
  arithmetic operations, performing
      with scalar 171
  dense vector 169
  elements, accessing 170
  element values, setting 170
  initializing 169
  sparse vector 169
vector space model (VSM)
  document indexing 207
  n-grams 208, 209
  normalization 209, 210
  text, preprocessing 205
  TF-IDF weighting 208

W

wrapper-based feature selection
  about 73
  backward selection 73
  forward selection 74
  recursive feature elimination 74

Thank you for buying
Learning Apache Mahout

About Packt Publishing

Packt, pronounced 'packed', published its first book, *Mastering phpMyAdmin for Effective MySQL Management*, in April 2004, and subsequently continued to specialize in publishing highly focused books on specific technologies and solutions.

Our books and publications share the experiences of your fellow IT professionals in adapting and customizing today's systems, applications, and frameworks. Our solution-based books give you the knowledge and power to customize the software and technologies you're using to get the job done. Packt books are more specific and less general than the IT books you have seen in the past. Our unique business model allows us to bring you more focused information, giving you more of what you need to know, and less of what you don't.

Packt is a modern yet unique publishing company that focuses on producing quality, cutting-edge books for communities of developers, administrators, and newbies alike. For more information, please visit our website at www.packtpub.com.

About Packt Open Source

In 2010, Packt launched two new brands, Packt Open Source and Packt Enterprise, in order to continue its focus on specialization. This book is part of the Packt Open Source brand, home to books published on software built around open source licenses, and offering information to anybody from advanced developers to budding web designers. The Open Source brand also runs Packt's Open Source Royalty Scheme, by which Packt gives a royalty to each open source project about whose software a book is sold.

Writing for Packt

We welcome all inquiries from people who are interested in authoring. Book proposals should be sent to author@packtpub.com. If your book idea is still at an early stage and you would like to discuss it first before writing a formal book proposal, then please contact us; one of our commissioning editors will get in touch with you.

We're not just looking for published authors; if you have strong technical skills but no writing experience, our experienced editors can help you develop a writing career, or simply get some additional reward for your expertise.

Apache Mahout Cookbook

ISBN: 978-1-84951-802-4   Paperback: 250 pages

A fast, fresh, developer-oriented dive into the world of Apache Mahout

1. Learn how to set up a Mahout development environment.

2. Start testing Mahout in a standalone Hadoop cluster.

3. Learn to find stock market direction using logistic regression.

Hadoop Real-World Solutions Cookbook

ISBN: 978-1-84951-912-0   Paperback: 316 pages

Realistic, simple code examples to solve problems at scale with Hadoop and related technologies

1. Solutions to common problems when working in the Hadoop environment.

2. Recipes for (un)loading data, analytics, and troubleshooting.

3. In depth code examples demonstrating various analytic models, analytic solutions, and common best practices.

Please check **www.PacktPub.com** for information on our titles

Scaling Apache Solr

ISBN: 978-1-78398-174-8   Paperback: 298 pages

Optimize your searches using high-performance enterprise search repositories with Apache Solr

1. Get an introduction to the basics of Apache Solr in a step-by-step manner with lots of examples.

2. Develop and understand the workings of enterprise search solution using various techniques and real-life use cases.

3. Gain a practical insight into the advanced ways of optimizing and making an enterprise search solution cloud ready.

Building Hadoop Clusters [Video]

ISBN: 978-1-78328-403-0   Duration: 02:34 hours

Deploy multi-node Hadoop clusters to harness the Cloud for storage and large-scale data processing

1. Familiarize yourself with Hadoop and its services, and how to configure them.

2. Deploy compute instances and set up a three-node Hadoop cluster on Amazon.

3. Set up a Linux installation optimized for Hadoop.

Please check **www.PacktPub.com** for information on our titles